Different Members, One Body

This resource has been developed in response to Overture 95–46, the 207th General Assembly (1995)

Resolved, That the Presbytery of Northern New York Overture the 207th General Assembly (1995) to do the following:

1. Affirm and proclaim the commitment of the Presbyterian Church (U.S.A.) to providing

    a. basic tools of ministry in alternative modes of communication to the printed word, for example braille, tape and computer technology, and signing;

    b. accessible meeting places;

    c. translation in the languages of congregations and sister churches with whom we are in mission partnership (where possible).

2. Initiate a study (through a commission appointed at the direction of the General Assembly Council that will include persons who are disabled) to

    a. determine the extent and variety of services needed, which shall include an accurate current assessment of the number of persons with disabilities—especially ministers, elders, and church professionals—who require such services in the rendering of their ministries;

    b. ascertain sources in society for providing such services as are needed, to explore patterns of present and potential cooperation with secular agencies, and to investigate the costs and means of funding such services;

    c. develop a process for identifying Presbyterian braillists and others who could contribute their skills in technologies of alternative communications and accessibility;

    d. report its findings to the 209th General Assembly (1997).

[3. Require that all materials; or a suitable summary thereof—minutes, resources, curriculum, etc.—produced by the Presbyterian Church (U.S.A.) shall be made available, when requested and in a timely fashion, in one or more of the following alternative formats—large print, audiocassette, braille, or computer disk, with expenditures not to exceed $50,000.

4. Through the General Assembly Council, determine an adequate budget for the above-mentioned commission's work and seek grants from foundations to help support the work of this commission.]

(Concurrence of Overture 95–46 from the Presbytery of the Western Reserve.)

DIFFERENT MEMBERS ONE BODY

Welcoming the Diversity of Abilities in God's Family

Edited by Sharon Kutz-Mellem

Witherspoon Press
Louisville, Kentucky

© 1998 Witherspoon Press, Presbyterian Church (U.S.A.), Louisville, KY

Unless otherwise indicated, Scripture quotations in this publication are from the New Revised Standard Version (NRSV) of the Bible, copyright © 1989 by the Division of Christian Education of the National Council of Churches in the U.S.A. Used by permission.

Every effort has been made to trace copyrights on the materials included in this book. If any copyrighted material has nevertheless been included without permission and due acknowledgment, proper credit will be inserted in future printings after notice has been received.

Grateful acknowledgment is made to Nancy Anne Dawe, Lydia Gans, and Crescent Hill Presbyterian Church, Louisville, Kentucky, for permission to reprint the photographs appearing on the cover and within the text.

Edited by Sharon Kutz-Mellem

Project Director: Cassandra D. Williams

Book interior and cover design by Claire Calhoun

First edition

Published by Witherspoon Press, a Ministry of the General Assembly Council, Congregational Ministries Division, Presbyterian Church (U.S.A.), Louisville, Kentucky, in partnership with the Commission on Enabling Ministry Services and the Office of the General Assembly.

PRINTED IN THE UNITED STATES OF AMERICA

98 99 00 01 02 03 04 05 06 07 — 10 9 8 7 6 5 4 3 2 1

Web site address: http://www.pcusa.org/pcusa/witherspoon

ISBN 1-57153-014-2

God has set each member of the body in the place
God wanted it to be. If all the members were alike, where
would the body be? There are, indeed, many different
members, but one body. The eye cannot say to the hand,
"I do not need you," any more than the head can say to
the feet, "I do not need you." Even those members of the
body which seem less important are in fact indispensable.

—1 Cor. 12:18–22 (paraphrased)

Alone we can do so little.
Together we can do so much.

—Helen Keller

Contents

Note: Diamonds (♦) and checkmarks (✔) indicate resources that provide step-by-step instructions for interacting with persons with disabilities.

Preface ix

Acknowledgments xi

Introduction 1
When Hesed Is the Norm
The Rev. John R. Sharp

1. Disability 101 3
Courtesy 3
Terminology 5
How to Interact with Persons with Disabilities . . . . 6 ♦
**What Can My Church Do
    to Learn More about Welcoming Persons with Disabilities?** . . . . 7 ✔
Additional Resources 8

2. Communication Access 9
Seeing the Word of God in New Ways 9
Hearing the Word of God in New Ways 11
Communicating the Word of God in New Ways 13
Converting Standard Print into Alternative Media . . . . 15 ♦
Working with Providers of Alternative Media 16
Guide Dogs and Assistance Animals 17
What Can My Church Do to Facilitate Communication Access? . . . . 18 ✔
Additional Resources 19

**3. Recognizing the Gifts of Persons with Developmental Disabilities,
Mental Retardation, Mental Illness, and Other Brain-based Illnesses** 23
A Place Called Acceptance
    Kathleen Deyer Bolduc 23
**What Can My Church Do
    to Welcome Children with Disabilities and Their Families?** . . . . 26 ✔

Mental Illness and Other Brain-based Illnesses 27

Before I Started to Serve
   Marcia A. Murphy 27

**What Can My Church Do
to Nurture the Gifts of Persons with Mental Illness?** . . . . 29 ✔

Additional Resources 30

4. Including Persons with Hidden Disabilities 31

Is She Really as Sick as She Says She Is?
   Kay Dawson Puckett 31

The Jeremiah Project
   Linda K. Reinhardt 32

What Can My Church Do to Live a Less Toxic Lifestyle? . . . . 34 ✔

Additional Resources 35

5. Removing Architectural Barriers 37

Where to Begin? 37

Universal Design . . . . 40 ◆

Accessibility Survey . . . . 41 ◆

How Can We Afford These Changes? 42

What Can My Church Do to Facilitate Removing Architectural Barriers? . . . . 44 ✔

Additional Resources 45

6. In Service to the Church—Embracing Our Workers 47

Fulfilling the Spirit of the Law . . . . 48 ◆

Hiring and Including Persons with Disabilities in Church Leadership 49

Seminary and Ordination Exams 49

Planning Accessible Meetings 50

**What Can My Synod, Presbytery, and Church Do
to Serve our Workers Who Become Disabled?**
   Dr. David Castrodale . . . . 52 ✔

Additional Resources 53

7. A Discussion about Disability 55

In God's Image
   The Rev. Sue Montgomery 55

Teaching a Church to "Be With"
   Brett Webb-Mitchell 57

Additional Resources 60

8. Resources of the Presbyterian Church (U.S.A.) 61

    Programs 61

    Services and Resources 62

9. Presbyterian Church (U.S.A.) Contacts and Resources by Synod 65

    Synod of Alaska/Northwest 65

    Synod of the Covenant 65

    Synod of Lakes and Prairies 67

    Synod of Lincoln Trails 68

    Synod of Living Waters 69

    Synod of Mid-America 69

    Synod of Mid-Atlantic 70

    Synod of the Northeast 71

    Synod of the Pacific 72

    Synod of Rocky Mountains 73

    Synod of South Atlantic 74

    Synod of Southern California and Hawaii 74

    Synod of the Southwest 75

    Synod of the Sun 75

    Synod of the Trinity 76

Notes 79

Glossary 81

Appendixes 83

    Appendix 1. The Americans with Disabilities Act (Pub. L. No. 101-336) 83

    Appendix 2. G.A. Overture 95–46 85

    Appendix 3. Biblical Languages: Learning Disabilities—Alternative Course of Study 87

    Appendix 4. Sample Registration Form 89

About the Commission Members and Staff 91

Preface

" "

If bars are more accessible than altars, if theaters are more welcoming than churches, if the producers of PBS are more sophisticated about communication access than our liturgists, if the managers of department stores know better how to appeal to those with disabilities than our church leadership, if the publishers of popular magazines are more knowledgeable about alternative formats than those who produce religious materials, then we have failed to meet Christ's challenge to us all.

—Mary Jane Owen[1]

" "

The Americans with Disabilities Act (ADA) was enacted into law in 1990. This law has been called the civil rights law for persons with disabilities. ADA holds our society accountable by law for discriminating against persons with disabilities. ADA's impact can be felt in all areas of public life, including public accommodations, employment, state and local government and its services, transportation, and even telecommunications. The law is broad, recognizing that disability by its very nature is broad and must be considered on a case-by-case basis. The church, with some exception, is not accountable under ADA. Instead, it *is* called to respond to the higher mandate of God, to faithfully fulfill the spirit of that law on a person-by-person basis.

Much could and already has been written about the failure of the institutional church to include persons with disabilities. Historically, the model has been to *minister to* rather than *minister with* persons with disabilities. Disability rights activists charge that the church is two decades behind the secular world when it comes to "getting it" about disability. The model has been to offer up pity and prayers for cure, rather than work to figure out how to change perceptual, attitudinal, and physical barriers in order to include persons with disabilities. At the very foundation of the model has been a failure to understand that regardless of the advances of medical science, disability will continue to exist; disability is a continuum on which we all reside—each of us is vulnerable either by circumstance, disease, accident, or age. The old model has been steeped in denial of the very fundamentals of our tradition as believers; that, disabled or able-bodied, we are all broken and sinful, we are all beautiful, we are all cherished members of God's family.

In spite of the historical facts and its failures and brokenness, the church has also listened to God's call and struggled to be faithful to that call. Sometimes quietly, churches, synods, presbyteries, and individuals have developed practical ways to include persons who do not read the printed word, who do not hear the spoken word, or who are not able to walk up the ten steps at the entrance of the sanctuary. Sometimes, not so quietly, we have taken the institutional church to task and called for action. At the 1995 General Assembly, Overture 95–46 (On Ministry Tools and Services for Persons with Disabilities), sponsored by the Presbytery of Northern New York, was approved. This overture, which was amended in 1996, asked the church to provide basic tools of ministry in alternative modes of communication to the printed word, accessible meeting places, and translation in the languages of congregations and sister churches. The overture also directed that a commission, which would include persons with disabilities, be established to determine the extent and variety of services needed, ascertain sources in society for providing such services, and develop a process for identifying Presbyterian braillists and others who could contribute their skills. The Commission on Enabling Ministry Services, supported by the Congregational Ministries Division, the Office of the General Assembly Council, and the Office of the General Assembly with staffing contributed by the National Ministries Division was created.

Stories about disability were solicited in a number of Presbyterian publications, including the every-household newspaper *Presbyterians,* produced by the General Assembly. Within these pages you will find these stories—examples of churches that have had successes, both large and small, in welcoming persons with disabilities. In order to use and celebrate the gifts of persons with disabilities, these churches have looked hard at their own hidden prejudices and fears, opening their hearts, minds, and checkbooks in order to find creative solutions to removal of barriers. You will also find suggestions from persons with disabilities or their family members and friends. They are the Presbyterian Church's true "experts" on welcoming the diversity of abilities in God's family and are our teachers for building a new partnership model of ministry.

The condition of disability requires honesty and intimacy, a willingness to ask for what is needed, and a willingness to listen and find solutions and ways to address those needs. Disability also requires flexibility. Because every church is unique and has its own unique needs, this book serves as a guide and not a definitive source for information concerning disability. Disability is addressed in very general terms. The terminology for disabilities is changing almost daily. Early references to disability that are quoted in this text are simply the accepted version of that word for that particular time period. (See chapter 1 for more on terminology.)

Some Suggestions for Using this Book

The stories and suggestions included are offered for your redesign—your own creative touches— and can be adapted to most situations, regardless of the nature of the disability. Permission is granted to use, extract, or copy material from this book with appropriate credit given. You may want to purchase a ring binder with divider pages. Photocopy the information you find here and organize it in a way that is most meaningful and useful to you. The resources appearing in this text are not an endorsement, but are merely suggestions that will further aid you in your ministry. Contact some of these sources and ask for additional information. File the information in your ring binder. Then devise some goals and objectives for improving ways your church can be more welcoming, along with a timeline for achieving your goals.

Use the information to develop a new evangelism strategy! There are an estimated 43 million persons with disabilities in the United States. How many of these persons attend your church? What ideas listed here can you replicate in your congregation in order to be able to share the good news with others?

Call or write some of your fellow Presbyterians listed in chapter 9. They can share their firsthand experiences about welcoming persons with disabilities. If you have experiences to share and were not identified on this list, please access the Presbyterian Church's Web site at www.pcusa.org. From this site, you can access the Commission on Enabling Ministry Services Web page by choosing "resources," or you can go directly to the site at http://www.members. xoom.com/cemusa. You may also write to Sharon Kutz-Mellem, 3630-A Brownsboro Rd., #203, Louisville, KY 40207.

Acknowledgments

Several weeks after placing the first announcement about this project in a Presbyterian publication, I went with some trepidation to my rented mailbox. I was afraid that I would find nothing, but was thrilled instead to find mail within days of the printing of that first announcement! And the letters and e-mail messages trickled in for months after, from members as far away as Puerto Rico and as near as my own congregation. It was to become a special time for me several days a week to check my mailbox and then return home to sit down with a pot of tea and read your thoughts, ideas, and suggestions about disability and our denomination. I hope you enjoyed our time together as much as I did! Thank you for caring enough about this issue to take the time to share your experiences and for your faithful witness and *hesed.*

I am grateful to the members of the Commission on Enabling Ministry Services and to Annie Wu King for all their positive support and for trusting me with this project, and for making my job a little easier. I appreciated their insight and suggestions.

I would be remiss if I did not express my appreciation to my mentors and teachers at *The Disability Rag:* Mary Johnson, Cass Irvin, and Julie Shaw Cole. Under their experienced tutelage, I learned new truths about disability as a culture and a community. These truths continue to aid me in my journey.

Note: The binding of this book is called Otabind and is one example of providing materials in alternative media. Because the pages of the book lie flat when the book is opened, it is easier to read for persons with some mobility limitations.

Introduction

ᶜᶜ ᵗᵗ

Hesed, translated from the Hebrew, "Abounding in kindness." Other possible translations are "abounding in steadfast love" (Revised Standard Version and New Revised Standard Version); "of great kindness" (King James Version); "rich in graciousness" (Jerusalem Bible); and "ever constant" (New English Bible).[1]

ᶜᶜ ᵗᵗ

When *Hesed* Is the Norm*

"Surely you are not suggesting that every single church has to be changed so it is barrier free: It just is not good stewardship." My friend and I were discussing our church's new building plans, plans that included a specific design that would provide persons with physical disabilities complete access. My friend went on to suggest there was no reason why a congregation couldn't refer persons with disabilities to other churches that were equipped. His comments struck me as strange, because our church is virtually barrier free, he supports all we have done in making it so, and a member of his own family will benefit from the efforts of those who developed and implemented plans to assure this access. Of course, I pointed out that such a "ministry by referral" meant not only turning away new members from churches that "referred," but also current members, many of whom had never known another church in their lives: those who were now infirmed by age,

those who were temporarily infirmed by injury, those whose eyesight had failed, those who were losing their hearing, and those who had lost their mobility. Moreover, since all of the above disabilities are physical, we must add to the list those who have developmental disabilities or mental disabilities—were they to be turned away also?

Nearly every pastor can point to just such faithful members within the congregation. But more than that, there are those who comprise 10 percent of our total population who will never be able to visit our churches unless we move beyond "ministry by referral" and realize that we are being watched and judged, as we speak of evangelism and justice in the same breath. I want to suggest that it is poor stewardship and poor theology to ignore, refer, or in any way contribute to the stigma that makes such persons "invisible" to our congregations. We desperately need churches that are committed to removing the "attitudinal barriers" that prevent persons from feeling part of the church family. Exclusion is an insidious process; no one ever sets out to build a church and/or church family that excludes—it just happens that way, unless there are intentional plans to prevent it.

Harold Wilke, founder and director of the Healing Community, who has lived with a physical disability since birth, notes in his book *Creating the Caring Congregation* that the major problem underlying all issues of accessibility is attitude. As with my friend, quoted above, the emphasis is on architecture—and architectural costs—when all along the real issue is attitude. The cost that is overlooked is the cost of an attitude of exclusion. In a church that is committed to justice and concerned about evangelism and outreach, what will it take

---

*The Rev. John Sharp, author of these comments, is pastor of Govens Presbyterian Church in Baltimore, Maryland. Govens has a long and rich history of shared ministry with persons with disabilities.

before we are conscious of the invisible multitudes in our midst, of individuals who want to be included and yet are overlooked because all we see is the disability and not the person?

In fairness to my friend, who opened this chapter with his disclaimer that not all churches can serve all the needs of persons with disabilities, there is some truth in his assessment that a single congregation could be overwhelmed if it tried to respond to all the needs of persons within the community who had physical and mental disabilities. There are specialty congregations, such as the local United Methodist congregation for the hearing impaired. In that church, everything is done with signing. And yet, I want to suggest that a congregation that begins with an attitude of acceptance and openness will be amazed at how far it can go in establishing a setting and an atmosphere of openness and inclusivity. We need to begin here, before we start planning on delegating and referring. How do we do that?

Bruce Rowlinson, in his book *Creative Hospitality as a Means of Evangelism* (Lebanon, TN: Green Leaf Press, 1980), calls for the church to rediscover "Creative Hospitality" in its midst. He wonders why we tend to bury it. What he calls hospitality I refer to as the biblical norm of *hesed*—loving-kindness. The Revised Standard Version of the Bible calls it steadfast love. Other translations call it "mercy" or "kindness." Linguists who have studied the word have noted that it is always used in the context of a covenant relationship with God. This is the way that God relates to us as humans. As we live in that covenant relationship, God expects the same relationship between us, as brothers and sisters. I believe *hesed* is an appropriate norm for a congregation that seeks to work for justice and is concerned about evangelism among all the people. As a covenant community, *hesed* describes the mutual love and assistance expected within a congregation. Many of our churches pride themselves on their "warmth" and their "warm fuzzies." I believe these are symptoms of an underlying gift of the Holy Spirit to congregational life—*hesed*.

If the word is new to you, sit down and read again the story of Ruth. It is a story in which an outsider demonstrates *hesed* to the covenant community of Israel. As the story unfolds, the kindness Ruth shows Naomi overflows in Naomi's family, prompting the kinsman Boaz to show kindness to Ruth—as the family is enfolded in kindness toward one another, they become the very embodiment of God's *hesed* toward Israel and the family of faith. So intertwined is *hesed* in the actions of the story and God behind the scenes that the scholar notes that "'hesed' in the human scene is evidence of God's hesed, God's faithful magnanimity. . . . We can say that persons act as God in the story."[2]

Last summer, during a workshop on "Evangelism and Justice, Ministering to Persons with Disabilities," one mother, whose child has Down syndrome, told of a pastor who refused to baptize the child. A young minister struggling with multiple sclerosis told of being "released," although the Board of Pensions would have provided disability income, making it possible for the congregation and minister to continue together with additional help. Why do these things happen? Wilke says people are uncomfortable with those who are different. Through fear and ignorance, great harm is being done to those who need our love and acceptance, to those who have so much love and insight to share with us. And yet, in my own experience with a congregation that is not all that different from the one in which you worship and serve, I have discovered that if we nurture the warmth that is already present, help put faces and names to those in need around us, *hesed* springs fresh from within. Congregations can be warm and gracious examples of acceptance and justice.

And so I lift up to you, not the "oughts and shoulds" of the Bible, but this one guiding principle that will invariably keep us on the right path— "*hesed*." It refers to much more than just isolated acts of kindness towards others; it is in fact the magnanimity of God in our midst.

1

Disability 101

❝ ❞

From the moment I set foot in the church, I knew I had found a home. I had just moved to Beverly Hills, and on my first visit I was warmly greeted and encouraged to come back, which I did. Almost from the beginning, when it was clear I was struggling to hold the hymnal or open a door, someone would come forward without hesitation, without fanfare, and with respect. . . . Now I sing in the choir and someone else holds the music as I look on.

> —Leslie Barnard, member of
> Beverly Hills Presbyterian Church,
> Beverly Hills, California

❝ ❞

Under the Americans with Disabilities Act (ADA), disability is defined in the following manner:

- A physical or mental impairment that substantially limits one or more of the major life activities of an individual such as walking, speaking, or breathing;
- a record of such an impairment; or
- being regarded as having such an impairment.

As is true with the general public, 17 percent of the members of a religious congregation have one or more disabilities. For purposes of the ADA, the definition of disability is very broad-based, and includes, among others, mobility and sensory impairments, mental illness, mental retardation, and learning disabilities. This definition of disability includes diabetes, cancer, HIV/AIDS, arthritis, as well as respiratory, cardiac, and physical conditions, such as chronic back pain.[1]

NANCY ANNE DAWE

The 203rd General Assembly (1991) adopted the phrase "Persons with Disabilities" and defined it as:

> A diverse group of individuals who have a physical or mental impairment which substantially limits one or more major life activity, such as relating, caring for one's self, performing manual tasks, walking, seeing, hearing, speaking, breathing, learning and working.[2]

Courtesy

Courtesy when welcoming persons with disabilities is really not very different from that of welcoming any person: a warm and genuine smile followed by a sincere greeting will usually get the ball rolling. The Rev. Stella Dempski is associate pastor of First United Presbyterian Church in Westminster, Maryland. Her experiences as a clergy member and professional in the field of disability as well as having lived life as a person with a disability makes her uniquely qualified to speak to the issue of the church and disability. When it comes to welcoming persons with disabilities, she says, "The larger problem is that the entire church tends to see people with disabilities as having something wrong with them, rather than (seeing) what abilities and gifts does this person have." She suggests that when we meet

NANCY ANNE DAWE

someone with a disability for the first time, we focus on ability rather than disability. Think about what is kind and unkind when interacting and become more sensitive to the language we use. At her church, the standard invitation, "All rise," is amended to "all those who are able, please stand."[3]

Courtesy also involves helping longtime members who develop disabilities later in life due to accident, illness, or the natural process of aging to continue to feel welcomed. Courtesy may require that we extend pastoral care or a compassionate hand, checking our pity at the

door. Such compassionate courtesy requires us to be creative and to respectfully find new ways for our members to serve and remain faithful. It may direct us to provide child care to a new mother who has just given birth to a child with a disability so that *she* can still serve on the finance committee. It may call us as a congregation to reassess the layout of our sanctuary to provide access to a member who now uses a wheelchair so that he can still attend worship and also *still* serve as usher on Sunday morning.

Respectful and courteous interactions require that we not talk down to persons with disabilities. There is no need to raise our voice when speaking to a person who uses a wheelchair, unless she is also hard of hearing. A person who is deaf or who does not speak is usually capable of understanding things at the same intellectual level as his or her peers, as long as we communicate in a "language" that he or she understands. Barb Robbins, a vacation Bible school teacher at First Presbyterian Church in Iron River, Michigan, and a person with hearing loss, finds most curriculum for deaf children woefully inadequate. Reviewing materials for her preschool class, she says, "(We) consider this material to be syrupy and an insult to the intelligence of the preschool kids we'll have. The program does try to introduce sign language, but again, it's much less than these kids are capable of understanding."

Nancy Unks and her husband Ralph are members of First Presbyterian Church in Springfield, Pennsylvania. Ralph was severely disabled nearly twenty years ago by a cerebral hemorrhage. Nancy adds this about welcoming persons with disabilities:

> I could offer much advice to churches on overcoming the physical barriers to inclusion— things that are not included in local building codes, which seem to be mostly written by nonhandicapped people. However, the most important is "Don't be afraid." Don't be afraid to approach, to mention the disability, to ask how you can help, to broach the tough spiritual "why" questions, to pray for healing even after years of disability, to offer the love and eternal hope that we have in Jesus Christ.

Terminology

Basic courtesy when meeting persons with disabilities begins with paying attention to terminology and how to refer to a person and a particular disability. On the issue of language, Brett Webb-Mitchell, assistant professor in Christian nurture at Duke University Divinity School, says that "the terms change yearly, if not daily. The persons, by the way, remain the same, but the labeling changes. The American Association of, now, Mental Retardation, in the 1980s was then the American Association on Mental Deficiency. They now have had nine or ten different definitions of mental retardation."[4]

Phrases such as "wheelchair bound" are no longer acceptable—many persons who use wheelchairs consider their chairs symbols of freedom and a primary means of access to the world, not a symbol to evoke pity. The word *handicapped* is demeaning to many persons because it brings to mind the image of a beggar with cup in hand or other negative images. Many people with disabilities feel "handicapped" only by the perceptual, attitudinal, and architectural barriers that they must face daily in the world. Some people with disabilities refer to their disability as a physical challenge. These changes in terminology are evidence of the level of empowerment that people with disabilities have achieved. We have become strong enough to tell others what we do and do not want to be called, even though we often can not agree among ourselves what we want to be called! The authors of *That All May Worship* caution, however:

> People with disabilities should acknowledge sincere efforts to change old language habits. "Politically correct" disability language is often presented in an overly oppressive way. As a result, people without disabilities, but with good intentions, may decide that trying to affirm and include people with disabilities isn't worth the effort.[5]

One important word guides all conversation regarding terminology—dignity.

> Language used to describe people with disabilities often focuses on lack of ability rather than on competency. Age-old terms such as "deaf and dumb," "invalid," or "idiot" continue to be used despite their disrespectful tone and the inaccurate message they portray. . . . When writing or speaking about people with disabilities, words should be chosen with care in order to promote dignity and a positive image.[6]

LYDIA GANS

Choosing "people first" language, and remembering that the disability is really not central to who that person is, is an important first step.

A brochure from the Research and Training Center on Independent Living and Paraquad, Inc.,[7] offers these additional tips:

- Make reference to the person first, then the disability. Say "a person with a disability" rather than "a disabled person."
- If the disability isn't germane to the story or conversation, don't mention it.
- A person is not a condition; therefore, avoid describing a person in such a manner. Don't present someone as "an epileptic." Rather say, "a person with epilepsy."
- Do not portray successful people with disabilities as superhuman, as this raises expectations that all disabled people should reach this level.
- Do not sensationalize a disability by use of such terms as "afflicted with," "victim of," "suffers from."
- Do not use generic labels for disability groups, such as "the retarded."
- The following terms should be avoided because they have negative connotations and evoke pity:

abnormal	maimed	spastic
burden	moron	stricken
deformed	palsied	stricken with
disformed	pathetic	suffer
incapacitated	pitiful	tragedy
imbecile	poor	unfortunate

How to Interact with
Persons with Disabilities*

A disabling condition often imposes isolation and loneliness on the person living with the condition. Therefore, it is particularly important that we not increase this loneliness by our unwillingness to engage in social interaction with persons who have disabilities. If you are wary or fearful, you may assume that the stranger in the wheelchair or with the white cane or with bilateral hearing aids feels the same way. In fact, you may assume that he or she feels and reacts the same way you do in almost all situations and that he or she has similar needs and interests and hopes. Try to focus on the person and remember:

Persons who have disabilities may not do the routine tasks of daily life in the same way that you do, but most of them can perform these tasks. Watch and learn. Be sincere and appropriate with your feedback. Everyone enjoys praise, but most adults do not want to receive praise for tying their shoes or zipping their zippers.

Ask a person who is disabled whether she wants or needs assistance. Don't begin by pushing or leading or helping.

Don't raise your voice to someone who is blind. His disability is loss of sight, not loss of hearing.

Difficulty with speech does not imply retardation. The person may have cerebral palsy, hearing loss, or numerous other conditions.

The majority of people with mental retardation function quite adequately in social situations and can carry on meaningful conversations. Before jumping to conclusions, have several conversations with a person.

To someone who is paralyzed or who has severe cerebral palsy, the wheelchair is a tool for independence; white canes and hearing aids fall into the same category. Be careful to avoid using words such as "wheelchair bound," "confined to wheelchair," and so forth.

Speak directly to a person who is disabled, rather than relying on an interpreter. In very few instances will she be unable to communicate for herself.

Don't be afraid to use sensory words such as "see" with a blind person, "hear" with someone who has a hearing impairment, or "feel" with someone who has neurological damage or some other condition that makes it impossible for him to feel. Most persons who have disabilities are quite comfortable using these words and find it an obvious strain on communication when you stumble with them.

Many persons who have disabilities know that they have found acceptance when you feel comfortable letting them know how you really feel about them. It's not a sin to dislike a disabled person.

Cut through your stereotypes by searching for the individual within. Being blind may have forced someone to hone his hearing skills, but it cannot in itself make him a good musician or a piano tuner. People who are blind do not have the gift of prophecy nor are they being punished for their sins with their blindness. All disabilities have some accompanying stereotypes that must be broken down.

Persons with disabilities are not "sick" people. Don't be afraid to touch someone with a disability; none of these conditions are contagious!

Allow disabled people to take responsibility for their lives, just as you want to do with your own life.

Don't be afraid to ask questions. How can you get to know people unless you ask them questions about themselves? Take your cue from the way small children interact with persons who have disabilities: They ask, and as a result, communication and social interaction go more smoothly.

Expect the same kind of give-and-take and sharing of roles in your relationship with someone who is disabled as you would in your other relationships. Treat the person who is disabled as your equal, rather than as the center of attention. Balance is the key to success in all successful relationships.

All of us have disabilities. Believing this can be a way of building community, but it should never be an excuse for ignoring the special needs of persons whose disabilities are more obvious. One special need is the use of specific and graphic language in directing someone who is blind. Rather than saying, "The library is right over there," say, "The library is about fifty feet to your left."

Don't "talk over" or provide the words for someone who stutters or speaks with difficulty. Be a good listener and allow her to say what she has to say. It is always permissible to feed back the sentence to make sure you have understood correctly.

Always face a person with a hearing impairment. Be sure the person can see your lips, and speak clearly without exaggerating lip movements. Many persons with hearing impairments are fairly adept as lip readers.

*Reprinted with permission from Barbara Ramnarine and Mary Jane Steinhagen, *AccessAbility: A Manual for Churches* (St. Paul, MN: Diocesan Office on Ministry with Persons Who Are Disabled of the Episcopal Diocese of Minnesota and Office for People with Disabilities, Catholic Charities of the Archdiocese of St. Paul, MN, 1997), pp. 10–11.

✔✔✔

What Can My Church Do to Learn More about Welcoming Persons with Disabilities?

1. The PCUSA Planning Calendar sets aside one Sunday a year to celebrate and recognize persons with disabilities. Its official title is Access Sunday. Take advantage of this date every year to educate your church about basic disability courtesy and issues or set another date on your own church's calendar. A packet of planning materials is available from Presbyterians for Disabilities Concerns (PDC), a network of the Presbyterian Health Education and Welfare Association (PHEWA), at 100 Witherspoon St., Louisville, KY 40202; phone: (502) 569-5800, or fax: (502) 569-8034.

2. Invite members of the congregation who have disabilities and speakers from local disability groups to come and educate the members of your adult and youth church school classes.

3. Identify churches from other denominations in your community that have had successes in including persons with disabilities. Use their expertise in developing a plan for including persons with disabilities.

4. Ask an architect, engineer, or other

> THIS IS MY COMMANDMENT, THAT YOU LOVE ONE ANOTHER AS I HAVE LOVED YOU.
>
> —JOHN 15:12

person who is experienced in access design to hold a workshop with your session or finance committee. She or he can walk members through your building, pointing out ways to make the building more accommodating to persons with disabilities.

5. If you already have an active disabilities committee in your congregation, ask them to hold a presbyterywide *teach-in*; provide a table of useful disability resources at presbytery meetings or at any other presbytery gathering. If you don't have such a committee, try to establish one.

6. As a congregation, spend a period of time prayerfully examining your church's mission, honestly checking for strengths and weaknesses when it comes to including persons with disabilities. Then devise a long-range plan for improving on the weak areas.

7. Make use of your presbytery's resource center for ideas, curriculum, videos, and other materials about disability. For a location near you, call PresbyTel at 1-800-872-3283.

AccessAbility: A Manual for Churches is a user-friendly book for congregations produced jointly by the Diocesan office on Ministry with Persons Who Are Disabled of the Episcopal Diocese of Minnesota and the Office for People with Disabilities, located within Catholic Charities of the Archdiocese of St. Paul–Minneapolis. Rich with resources and helpful comments by persons with disabilities. The cost is $10.00. Contact: Rev. Barbara Ramnaraine, St. James on the Parkway, 3225 East Minnehaha Parkway, Minneapolis, MN 55417. Toll-free: 1-800-440-1103; phone: (612) 721-1103.

The Center for Ministry with People with Disabilities of the University of Dayton has a number of videotapes and print publications for ministry with people with disabilities. Titles included on the video list are *Disability Etiquette*, a training video for interaction with people with disabilities, and *Welcome One, Welcome All*, which demonstrates the process for teaching the gospel around children with disabilities. They also produce a handy brochure called *Welcoming People with Disabilities: Do's & Don'ts for Parish Ministers*. The cost is $1.00, with bulk discounts for orders of 20 or more. For ordering information and a complete price list and catalog, contact: Network of Inclusive Catholic Educators, University of Dayton, Dayton OH 45469-0317. Phone: (937) 229-4325; fax: (937) 229-3130.

SEMAR (Southeastern United Methodist Agency for Rehabilitation, Inc.) produces a packet of materials for the local church to aid it in ministry with persons with disabilities. In addition to "Information for Ushers and Greeters," the packet contains Disability Awareness Sunday materials, how to conduct an Accessibility Audit in your church, and more. Cost for postage, handling, and the packet is $7.00. Send your check and request for PACKET to: SEMAR, Inc., P.O. Box 128, Lake Junaluska, NC 28745. For additional information, call (toll-free) 1-800-527-3627; TDD: (704) 452-7640; and Voice: (704) 452-2881, ext. 732/734.

Surprising Grace: People, Disabilities, Churches is a fifteen-minute videotape with study guide produced by PDC and Media Services, Congregational Ministries Division, PC(USA). The video includes interviews with persons who have a variety of disabilities, discussing the gifts they contribute to their churches and why persons with disabilities feel welcomed by their churches. The cost is $5.00. To order, call the Presbyterian Distribution Center at 1-800-227-2872 and ask for PDS# 72-650-98-001.

The United Church Board for Homeland Ministries (United Church of Christ) has a resource packet that was developed by the National Committee for Persons with Disabilities. The packet includes an information sheet, "Points to Remember When You Meet a Person with a Disability." For ordering information, contact Barbara T. Baylor, Minister for Health and Welfare Programs, or Rev. David Denham, United Church Board for Homeland Ministries, 700 Prospect Ave., Cleveland, OH 44115-1100. Phone: (216) 736-3272.

That All May Worship: An Interfaith Welcome to People with Disabilities is a handbook with a common-sense approach to assisting congregations in welcoming persons with disabilities. The cost is $10.00 (multicopy discounts available). Contact: National Organization on Disability (NOD), Religion and Disability Program, 910 16th St., N.W., Ste. 600, Washington, DC 20006. Phone: (202) 293-5960; fax: (202) 293-7999; TDD: (202) 293-5968.

2

Communication Access

❝ ❞

I returned from the 1991 General Assembly in Baltimore a grieved, disappointed, and determined pastor. . . . Despite assurances . . . that the opening Communion service would be in braille, and that all one would have to do was to ask for a copy, it wasn't—ushers couldn't find them because they hadn't been brailled. I had to suppress the tears of sadness and anger at not being able to share in responses, hymns, prayers, and the liturgy of our Lord's Supper because I couldn't read them in a mode that had been my language through thirty-seven years of ministry.

> —Rev. William Richard Jr., retired
> Presbyterian minister, Vergennes, Vermont

❝ ❞

Seeing the Word of God in New Ways

Blindness and Visual Disabilities

Access to communication among persons who do not use standard print (sometimes called regular print) materials is critical to those persons' ability to participate fully in the life of the church. Access to materials is not just restricted to Sunday morning worship, but also to committee minutes and announcements, reports, and other important documents of the church. The format in which this material is produced is based on a very specific level of need: Not every person who is blind reads braille. One might depend on large-print copy or audiocassette tapes and one might take full advantage of every technological device available. Providing accessible materials is often on a case-by-case, as-requested basis.

Rick Roderick, an ordained Presbyterian minister, has been blind since birth. He reads braille. Braille is a system of raised dots on paper and is available in several grades, although two grades of braille are most commonly used: Grade I braille uses regular punctuation but no contractions; Grade II braille uses regular punctuation along with contractions. Grade II braille is also known as standard English braille and is the format most commonly available commercially. Braille pages are usually produced in interpoint braille— embossed on both sides of the page. Single-sided braille, pages embossed on one side, is also available commercially. Most early home braille embossers were designed to print single-sided braille. The advantage of double-sided braille is that about twice the amount of material can be brailled on one sheet, making the weight and size of the document less and a little easier to handle. A standard braille page is usually the equivalent of two standard print pages. Commercial providers will quote a price per page based on a standard braille page.

As a part of his duties as an assistant technology specialist and braille transcriber for the Kentucky Department for the Blind, Rick stays aware of all the current technology that is important to persons who are blind, but acknowledges that not all persons who read braille are interested in new technology. He uses his knowledge of technology to educate his church, Crescent Hill Presbyterian Church in Louisville, Kentucky, and his presbytery. He owns both a computer with a modem and a

braille embosser. The weekly Sunday bulletin is sent to him by his church's secretary over her computer modem so he can have it in hand on Sunday morning. Committee reports and notices are also sent to him in this manner by the secretary, but more often—thanks to the proliferation of home computers with modems, materials are sent by other people who serve with him on the committees. When a modem is not available, materials are given to him on computer diskettes. With the aid of special computer software, Rick formats the material into braille, which is then printed by his embosser. He has made information such as the Sunday bulletin available on an "as requested" basis to others who attend his church and also read braille.

Timothy Little, manager of the pastoral care services at the University of California—Davis Medical Center in Davis, California, is also legally blind. At times during his life he has had some vision. His main means of access to standard print during his nonvision periods is a Kurzweill Reader. The reader functions like a scanner or photocopier. A document is placed on the reader, the material is scanned, and the characters are recognized and then converted to

voice. Some persons with visual disabilities might use other equipment, like a magnifier. Magnifiers can range from the simple, hand-held magnifier costing only a few dollars to a closed-circuit TV magnification system which operates similarly to an overhead projector.

Tim and others with visual disabilities are sometimes able to read materials in large print. Large-print refers to the size of the type that appears on a printed page. Most books are printed in 10- or 12-point type. Large-print materials are usually 18-point type or larger. Increasing the size of print type can be managed easily on most computer programs these days. However, fancy fonts should be avoided, as these are often less clear and more difficult to read, and the same can be true of special formatting such as centered titles, columns, and italics. A standard copy machine can also be used to enlarge print by simply increasing the percentage to 150 percent or higher. Persons with low vision, or who are partially sighted, benefit from high contrast in their large-print materials. This can be achieved by using bold ink on white or yellow paper. Documents that are produced commercially in large print are usually large in size and have extra-wide bindings and margins. This allows the reader to press the volume flat to read or to use with visual aid equipment such as the Kurzweill Reader. Some persons prefer that their large-print materials be printed on standard-sized paper whenever possible because it is simply easier to manage than 8 1/2 x 11-inch paper.

It is not uncommon for persons who are legally blind but who have some vision to use a combination of tools in accessing the printed word, such as a magnifier with large print. However, according to Rick Roderick, most people consider audiocassette tape to be the most universal alternative format. Audiotape reaches persons with a variety of disabilities, including blindness and learning disabilities, as well as persons who may have disabilities that restrict their mobility or make it difficult to hold a book, or who might have chemical sensitivity to particular inks and paper. It is a format that is most often used by persons who become blind late in life, because they do not want to learn braille or may not be interested in learning new technology.

Hearing the Word of God in New Ways

Deafness and the Hard of Hearing

❝ ❞

My partner is deaf and joined the church over a year ago. Prior to joining, we were exploring and trying to use interpreters to sign the Sunday morning worship. The more we scheduled interpreters, the more excited people became and the more members appeared to embrace the entire movement toward inclusion. When the church recognized the need for a more inclusive service that reached across the communication barrier my partner became a member of this fine church.

> —Susan Slocum, member of First
> Presbyterian Church, Winnebago, Illinois

❝ ❞

People who are hard of hearing communicate through enhanced sound and lipreading (speech reading). Sound systems that serve everyone are important additions to the sanctuary and meeting rooms. But in order to be fully involved in worship and study, a person with partial hearing may benefit from an assistive listening device (ALD) such as a hearing aid, an audio loop worn around the neck, and a small microphone worn on the speaker's lapel.

People who are deaf prefer interpreted conversation using American Sign Language (ASL), signed English, or Cued Speech. Since ASL is a language with its own syntax allowing for the exchange of ideas on many levels, it forms the basis for what is known as the Deaf Culture.

Signing is a beautiful art form. It will greatly enrich the worship experience for all, once the congregation becomes accustomed to it. For many people who are deaf, however, it is more than an art form. It is the primary way to understand the full content of worship.

Many deaf people prefer to worship in a deaf congregation. Others seek a mainstream religious community which is able to arrange for sign language or oral interpretation of worship services and activities. This is particularly important for deaf parents who have hearing children and wish to worship as a family.[1]

As with blindness and vision impairment, there is also a wide range of communication options for persons who are deaf or hard of hearing. A person using a hearing aid may have great difficulty hearing in a large room such as a sanctuary when there is a lot of background noise or echo/reverberation. Options for improving sound quality include the use of assistive listening systems (ALS). ALS are devices that retrieve sound close to its source and amplify it to the listener while filtering out the background noise. Such systems can be *hardwired*—connected directly to the public address system and then transmitted to an individual headset that is powered off its own amplifier in a designated area or seat. An *induction loop system* allows hearing aid users to pick up an electromagnetic field generated by special wiring that encompasses the room. It is

NANCY ANNE DAWE

activated by an amplifier that gets its signal from the room's public-address system. These systems do not work well in rooms with movable walls because the signal becomes difficult to detect. In addition, fluorescent lights and strong motors (those used for refrigeration and elevators, for example), can affect the signal as well. Not all hearing aids have telephone switches that activate the induction coil, which in turn blocks room noise.

Radio frequency systems are portable (FM transistor radio) receivers with earphones and/or induction loops that are used by persons in the audience and transmitters that connect to the public-address system directly or via a small transmitter worn by the speaker. Signals from these systems work well outdoors and can pass through walls, and can be purchased with multiple channels to reach many rooms.

Infrared systems consist of a "light-emitting diode panel that is connected to the sound source. The panel broadcasts invisible infrared light out into the assembly space. Users carry small receivers with earphones." This system is not good for outdoor use, as the sun's rays interfere with the signal. The signal also will not pass between walls which is a plus when it comes to security or confidentiality.[2]

There are several modes of reception available for the listener with the ALS. The mode most commonly used by churches, according to Rick Roderick, is the single earphone. This works well for someone who has better hearing in one ear than the other. A second method uses a pair of headphones; many persons can hear better using both ears than one ear by itself. A third method is the use of a small loop that uses the coils or telephone switches in the hearing aids. This allows for greater amplification than earphones. Costs for an ALS depends on a number of variables, including the number of receivers and the size of the room. (See page 22 for several sources for ALS and similar equipment.)

Some people who are born deaf or become deaf early in life communicate by using sign language. Although American Sign Language (ASL) is most often used, there are a variety of other sign systems. ASL is expressed by finger and hand movements, gestures, and facial expressions and has its own vocabulary, grammar, and syntax. Qualified interpreters of sign language have received special training and can be licensed or certified depending on a particular state's requirements. The average cost per hour for a professional interpreter is between $25 and $40 per hour, with a two-hour minimum.[3]

Cindy Fuess, a sign language interpreter in Iowa, offers this additional information about her profession:

> As far as cost, that depends where you are. Around here in Iowa, I would say $10 to $15 an hour is acceptable. Some people will charge portal to portal, and use that time determining the cost. Personally, I never charge a church

because I consider it is part of a ministry. After about 20 minutes of straight interpreting, an interpreter needs a little break. Anything over 2 hours, you would want to "break" with another interpreter for sure. I have learned ways to "refresh" during the offertory, etc. If it is a meeting where a lot of people are talking, I would advise to have 2 interpreters at least.

Using a professional sign language interpreter is always preferable; Ms. Fuess acknowledges, however, that this is not always possible.

> Finding a "qualified" interpreter is not an easy task. Some cities have Deaf Services and/or Interpreter Referral Agencies. Many people do not feel comfortable doing church interpreting and/or are already involved in a church.

Some churches in our denomination have devised creative solutions to finding and providing professional interpreting services. Nobel Road Presbyterian Church in Cleveland Heights, Ohio, implemented a program to address the needs of persons with speech and hearing disabilities that includes regularly planned training in sign language as part of its mission. Youths, adults, and clergy are all involved in the learning process. Member Michael Barkoot writes, "My joy in all of this is in seeing our son experience the shrinking of his isolation, the increasing of his self-esteem and the growing opportunity to participate in the church and to achieve new understanding of what his faith journey is all about."

There is a broad range of perspectives regarding hearing loss. Some persons who are deaf view deafness as a culture with its own language (ASL) and a way of life to be cherished and celebrated, not as something that must be "fixed." Heritage Presbyterian Church in Lincoln, Nebraska, is a church that embraces the idea of Deaf Culture. It has hosted a worship service that featured a deaf preacher, a signing choir, and a children's story told with signing and mime. "This was a role reversal for the hearing community," reported the church's minister, Ray Meester. "Many hearing people reported that it was the most inspirational worship they'd ever experienced."[4] In addition to weekly signed Sunday worship services, Heritage Presbyterian also signs its session meetings, opens its doors to several secular deaf groups, and has hosted an ecumenical worship for church interpreters who speak ASL.

Persons who are deaf want to have access to the same materials that hearing persons, do and this includes audiovisual materials such as videotapes, television programs, and movies. Captioning is one way to ensure that persons who are deaf have access to such media. Two of the most common forms of captioning are closed captions and open captions. "Closed captions are captions, spoken words, and/or audio effects displayed as text, encoded or hidden on line 21 of the television signal. To see captions, one must have a decoder (costs vary between $100 and 200) installed on a television. The decoder opens the captions for viewing. . . . Open captions are visible to all viewers (without the use of a decoder)." By law, new television sets larger than thirteen inches and manufactured in the United States must have a decoder chip installed.[5]

Communicating the Word of God in New Ways

❝ ❞

Christmas is the season of perpetual hope, joy, and love.

—Jeremy, a participant in
 Hamburg Presbyterian Church's
 Christian Nurture Ministry
 with mentally retarded adults

❝ ❞

A learning disability (LD) is a permanent disorder which affects the manner in which individuals with normal or above average intelligence take in, retain, or express information. Like interference on the radio or a fuzzy TV picture, incoming or outgoing information may become scrambled as it travels between the eye, ear or skin, and the brain.[6]

Communication is more than hearing and seeing. It is also understanding and having access to materials that we can understand. Whenever possible, the best approach to teaching the word of God is to find ways to include persons who learn differently, not to

segregate them into a separate class or program. Communication and participation in worship and church school by persons with learning disabilities or developmental disabilities, and by others who do not read standard print or who may not be able to speak, requires a creative approach, based on individual need. Persons with these particular disabilities and their families are often the best sources of information on how to provide materials. The nature of these disabling conditions includes a wide range of needs and very specific ways of accessing materials. A learning disability, for example, is not a form of mental retardation or an emotional disorder. It usually is not a measure of a person's intelligence. It is, however, a disorder that may affect reading comprehension, spelling, written expression, and problem solving. In addition, a learning disability may be very inconsistent and vary from week to week. Individual modifications may need to be made to a church school curriculum in order to include a student with a learning disability, such as providing audiotaped lessons in advance of weekly church school.

Kathy Dudley, co-pastor of Sweetwater Presbyterian Church in Hickory, North Carolina, is the parent of a child who is autistic and old enough now to enter the youth class at his church. Kathy recognizes the difficulty in finding resources for persons with mental illness and social and emotional disabilities, and her concern is that her son and others will find it difficult to be included with others who are his chronological age. She writes:

> Our church has a high percentage of children with developmental disabilities in Sunday school, worship, and Bible school. We are just doing it, with a few ideas and no training. . . . Involving such children in our regular programs, sometimes at a level behind their chronological age, has worked quite well, with no extra expenses. We do find that assistants are needed in several classes, even though our classes are small (4–8 students).

Some persons who have retardation are able to read, write, and understand everything that is happening in worship and church school. For persons who do not, communication can be handled by a multisensory approach that concentrates on hearing, seeing, touching, tasting, smelling, and movement. Chaplain Margot Hausmann of the Eastern Christian Children's Retreat in Wyckoff, New Jersey, has compiled an extensive list, which includes the following ideas:

Kinesthetic Elements

Clapping with hands, feet, *and* eyes! Dance and expressive dance movements with arms or legs as able; processions to site of worship with banners, placards, wheelchairs, music, etc. Raising of the eyes as praise or to ask for God's help; gestural leadership, as congregation follows the leader's gestures (posture, arms, etc.).

Auditory Elements

Greeting each person by name; speaking the names of participants often (e.g., "God so loved the world, Helen, that he gave his only son [for us], Richard"); responsive readings that allow a congregation or assistant leader to participate with a simple response.

Visual Elements

Colorful banners appropriate to the message, also use of simple symbols such as arrows pointing up or down; slides projected onto screen corresponding to each part of the service (e.g., Bible, offering plate, praying hands); stole and paraments of season's liturgical color, also point out others present wearing color. When celebrating the priesthood of all believers, crepe-paper stoles for all!

Tactile Elements

Greeting and gently touching each person as service begins; anointing of hand/forehead with oil; lotion can be rubbed on hands; laying on of hands as participants receive a prayerful blessing. Depending on comfort level: gentle touch on arm, hand on head, hands on shoulders, or embracing sides of head, with hands.

Olfactory Elements

Scented anointing oil on hand/forehead; incense as a reminder of God's presence in the temple; baking bread from portable bread-making machine

Gustatory Elements

Eucharist, receive bread, juice; can be served to all as a taste of pabulum with grape juice, or in the Russian Orthodox tradition of breaking the bread into the cup and spooning it into mouth;

tastes of honey, bitter herbs, and other illustrative flavors.[7]

Hamburg Presbyterian Church in Hamburg, New York, has launched a ministry that augments Christian education and is an outreach to residents in local group homes for adults with mental retardation. The ministry was begun in 1995 as a way to provide worship for a member's brain-injured son who was unable to participate in regular Sunday morning services. Member Sue Earle writes,

> When we began this ministry, we contacted the chaplain at the state developmental center near us. Her suggestions for ministering to people with mental retardation were most helpful. We also approached the local ecumenical council of churches to offer our assistance with starting a program in other churches in Hamburg.

Ms. Earle suggests that the order of worship for the service remain the same from week to week. This allows members of the congregation to become familiar and comfortable with worship. Although Hamburg now uses a curriculum series called "Friendship," they relied on visual aids—ordinary objects or pictures or videos—during the first years of their ministry. The local Hamburg beach was used, for example, to shoot videotape of rock and sand. The videotape was used to tell the Bible story of the wise man and the foolish man (visual). Rocks and sand were also passed around so everyone could touch (tactile and visual), and a song about the wise man building his house on the rock was sung (auditory).

Connecting with other resources in the community or other denominations within a community may also be helpful to purchase or share adaptive equipment for persons who do not speak. Nancy Unks writes about the efforts to aid her husband Ralph in communicating:

> Our church was joined by other churches in the community in an ecumenical campaign to raise the money for the Eyegaze Computer System, which enables him to communicate. Our inclusion in the life of the church has not been the result of any organized ministry or program. It's only because individuals took the time to care and made the effort to communicate, since Ralph can't initiate communication himself.

Converting Standard Print into Alternative Media

Production issues and related costs facing a church that wants to include persons with a variety of communication access needs may initially seem staggering. The following suggestions are designed to take some of the mystery out of providing materials in alternative media:

Always ask specific questions of the person for whom you are providing materials. He or she may have some good solutions. Don't forget, also, to network in your congregation and your community. Think ecumenically and you might be able to find someone in another denomination with expertise in sign language, for example, who may worship at a time different from your congregation and can sign for your service for free or for a small donation.

The least problematic and least expensive form of alternative medium is to provide materials via computer by modem or on computer diskette. This, however, requires the initial expense of the equipment and requires that the person who needs alternative media also has the appropriate equipment.

Contact your local independent living center or rehabilitation center for suggestions. Hospital social service units and state rehabilitation departments are another good source. All these sources will have contacts in the community who volunteer or sell alternative media services. Look in your yellow pages and find listings for local chapters of national organizations for persons who are blind, deaf, or who have other disabilities.

Consider the number of persons for whom you are providing the materials. If you have only four persons in your presbytery who read braille, it is not necessary to print twenty copies of the *Book of Order* in braille.

When recording material on cassette, the method can be as unsophisticated (and inexpensive) as using conventional recording equipment and a volunteer, or can employ commercial recording and duplicating services. When using the former method, the volunteer reader should have a clear recording voice and read at a moderate speed. The recording should be done in a quiet room with no background noise. At the beginning of the tape, the reader should identify herself or himself and the name of the document that is being read, as well as citing the page number(s) of what is being read and identifying which side of the tape the reader is using (for example, "This is tape 1, side 1, *Different Members, One Body*, pages 12 through 15, Amanda Scharf reading").

If you are considering contracting out audiotape needs, understand that two very separate components are involved: creating a master (recording the original) and duplicating (producing the individual cassettes), which will involve thinking about packaging and mailing. Be advised that most commercial duplicating services have a minimum order of 500 to 600 cassettes. It may be more cost effective to solicit volunteer help from your local radio station for the studio time and reader in order to make a master tape, then make a few cassette copies using standard, tape-to-tape home recording equipment or contracting with a separate duplicating company.

Volunteer providers are wonderful sources, but because they are volunteers they may have lengthy turnaround times and are not always able to set a deadline for return of their work. Timeliness of materials is a critical issue that must be considered: Brailled materials arriving on the last day of General Assembly or not at all do not allow an attendee to participate fully.

Publicize or otherwise make it known that you can provide materials in alternative media on an "as requested" basis, or set within your budget monies to provide one form of alternative medium that will reach the greatest number of persons, such as audiotape. Providing materials routinely in alternative media also has the hidden benefit of bringing new members to your church's door!

Working with Providers
of Alternative Media

In addition to the number of copies, details about how you will provide the material that is to be brailled (via the Internet, by fax, or on a computer diskette, for example), cost, and the expected date the job will be completed, a braillist may also have some options available for binding the materials and providing covers. He may want to know if a braille label is needed, and he may have a number of packaging or envelope options. He will also need mailing/delivery instructions. Will the material be delivered by first-class mail, an express mail delivery service, or by Free Matter? *Free Matter* is one option offered by the United States Postal Service for persons with disabilities to receive materials free of postage costs. It does require that the sender have a special permit, and a number of qualifications must be met in order to get this permit. If multiple copies are ordered, your braillist will also want to know if the items are going to be shipped to more than one address and, if so, to whom?

Commercial recording and duplication services, whether they charge fees or provide volunteer services, may have a choice in recording and duplication options such as two-track or four-track tapes. The advantage of four-track tapes over two-track is that the former are recorded at a slower speed and four times as much material can be recorded onto the tape. The disadvantage of four-track tapes is that special equipment is required to play the tapes. This equipment can be purchased or borrowed, and both the Library of Congress and Recording for the Blind use four-track tape systems.

As mentioned earlier, providing material on audiotape consists of two components: creating a master copy and the duplication process. Usually, these operations are handled by two separate companies. There are a few companies, however, that can provide both the recording of the master and the duplication. Recording the master will require studio rental time and charges for an engineer. There will also be fees for a professional reader to make the master tape. Jim Baker of Magnetix, a commercial duplicating company in Florida, recommends using a professional reader because it is cheaper in the long run. A professional will make fewer mistakes and require less editing time, which will of course bring the cost down. He suggests that a good rule of thumb in calculating the length of studio time needed to make the master is to allow three times as much time as it takes to read a book (for example, if it takes six hours to read a standard print book, plan on eighteen hours of recording time with a professional reader). Recording for the Blind and other similar operations carefully match their volunteer readers with the material they are reading, based on their particular expertise in a chosen field or area. An attorney, for example, will read law books and a doctor will read medical journals or similar materials, because they are familiar with the terminology, special concepts related to their field, and correct pronunciation.

Once the master tape is recorded, tapes are duplicated and the cost is based on the number of feet of tape per cassette. The duplicator may also have choices regarding the type of packaging and labels and will also want delivery instructions. Duplicating companies may have a number of other options pertaining to the type of insert that goes inside the cassette case, whether or not the cassette label is to be brailled, and whether or not the cassette is to be shrink-wrapped, for example.

Ordering materials both in standard print and in alternative media may seem overwhelming, but once braille and providers of other alternative media are identified and you have set the terms of your agreement, the process becomes quite routine. It is even possible, with a little planning, to have your materials produced so that you have simultaneous distribution or mailing of your materials. Usually this means you will need to establish a production calendar that allows a few days of extra time for the production of braille or other alternative media and then the printing of your standard or regular print material to coincide with the date you plan to mail these materials or make them available to all the members of the congregation.

Guide Dogs and Assistance Animals

Persons with a variety of disabilities rely on guide dogs or assistance animals (sometimes called service animals) to aid them in navigating the way to communicating with others. Assistance animals are used by persons who are blind or who have visual disabilities to negotiate their physical surroundings. They can be used by persons who are deaf to alert them to sounds that cannot be heard, and they are even used to pull persons who use wheelchairs or to retrieve dropped items for persons who have restricted mobility. Assistance animals have the added benefit of serving as an icebreaker, stimulating contact by a person who otherwise may have been too reticent to approach a person with a disability. Nat Dean, a member of First Presbyterian Church in Sante Fe, New Mexico, has a head injury and uses an assistance dog. She says that the church has gone the extra mile in welcoming her and her dog, providing transportation for both as needed. "Everybody loves the dog, Binny, as she mingles at coffee time and special events and sits quietly at my feet in the third pew on Sunday during services," says Nat. Binny and Nat have even posed together in a photograph for the church's directory.

Although assistance animals are loved by their owners and are true companions, they are essentially working animals that have gone through extensive training to be able to respond to their owners' needs. Disability etiquette requires that we ask before we pet or distract these animals in any way. Their owners are usually delighted to accommodate you, but let them give their permission.

Manassas Presbyterian Church in Manassas, Virginia, is very aware of the value of assistance animals in improving the lives of persons with disabilities. It is a training site for guide dogs that are supplied by Guiding Eyes for the Blind. Families from the church have raised and trained puppies for over ten years. Members and puppy raisers Spence and Ann Curtis are volunteers with this organization. Once the puppies are ready for socializing, they attend nearly all the functions at Manassas Presbyterian Church. According to the Curtises,

> The premise of raising a guide dog puppy relates closely to what we are taught as Christians. When the puppy leaves, you have given a gift that means very much to you. You give it up for someone without sight who(m) you (know) nothing else about. It is difficult to let go and rewarding to see the puppy you loved and raised working as someone's eyes. My wife and I feel this has been one of the major ways we have taught our three children Christian love and to give of themselves. We know that without the welcome and encouragement of our church community we probably wouldn't still be at it.

LYDIA GANS

What Can My Church Do to Facilitate Communication Access?

1. Devise a plan of action that will make communication access intentional. This can be a step-by-step plan that implements change gradually and does not have to wreak havoc with your church's budget. For example, in year one make large-print copies of your church's bulletin and newsletter available and let the community know what you are doing. Year two, purchase several large-print hymnals and perhaps one in braille. Identify potential braille providers or volunteer readers and provide materials on an as-requested basis. Purchase teaching aids pertinent to assisting persons with learning disabilities or developmental disabilities. Year three, launch a capital campaign to remedy auditory problems, adding assistant hearing devices.

2. Several churches in one presbytery might consider pooling funds to purchase a braille embosser and a braille translation program. (*It is important to note that purchase of an embosser requires that someone have knowledge of its use, along with the software—an experienced braillist is critical.*) In this same vein, several churches might contribute funds to make materials available on audiocassette and to purchase teaching aids and materials for persons with learning disabilities or developmental disabilities or purchase other adaptive communications equipment. All could be made available through the presbytery's Learning Resource Center.

> ALL THE KINGS OF THE EARTH SHALL PRAISE YOU, O LORD, FOR THEY HAVE HEARD THE WORDS OF YOUR MOUTH.
>
> —Ps. 138:4

3. Build into your annual budget monies to make materials available in alternative media. Involve the whole congregation in fund-raising efforts—hold bake sales, yard sales, or find other creative ways to raise funds.

4. Send your alternative media needs to volunteer organizations or, better, identify someone in your community who has the necessary equipment to produce braille or audiocassettes.

5. Make sermons and other documents available in print for persons who are deaf or hard of hearing. The Rev. Norman Nettleton served a small congregation with limited resources before retirement and used to write the sermon title and a synopsis of the sermon on a 3 x 5–inch index card. These days, with most churches having access to a computer, sermons can be printed out for persons who do not hear or have hearing loss.

6. Several churches in a community might pool resources to purchase adaptive equipment or computer equipment and related software for persons who do not speak or who have mobility limitations that prevent their turning pages. Technology is moving at the speed of light, and newer and better equipment is available, with cost in some cases no longer prohibitive.

7. Curriculum Publishing of the PC(USA) will have its curriculum brailled, if requested. The church or individual requesting the braille is responsible for the cost of transcribing. Please call (800) 524-2612 for more information.

Additional Resources

Service and Assistance Animals

Dogs for the Deaf
    10175 Wheeler Rd.
    Central Point, OR 97502
    Toll-free: 1-800-990-3647
    E-mail:
    www.workingdogs.com
    Trains dogs for deaf persons

Guiding Eyes for the Blind
    611 Granite Springs Rd.
    Yorktown Heights, NY 10598
    Toll-free: 1-800-942-0149
    Phone: (914) 245-4024
    Fax: (914) 245-1609
    E-mail:
    info@guiding-eyes.org

Paws with a Cause®
    National Headquarters
    4646 South Division
    Wayland, MI 49348
    Toll-free: 1-800-253-PAWS
    (TDD/Voice)
    E-mail: www.ism.net
    Assistance dogs for people
    with disabilities

The Seeing Eye, Inc.
    P.O. Box 375
    Morristown, NJ 07963-0375
    Phone: (201) 539-4424
    Has listing of Guide Dog
    schools

Sources of Volunteer and Commercial Providers of Alternative Media

Library of Congress
    Washington, DC 20542
    Toll-free: 1-800-424-8567
    Ask for the free directory of
    volunteer groups and
    individuals who transcribe
    and record books and other
    reading materials for
    persons who are blind.

National Braille Press, Inc.
    88 St. Stephen St.
    Boston, MA 02115
    Phone: (617) 266-6160
    Fax: (617) 437-0456
    Call for a list of braille and
    audiotape providers.

National Library Service for the
    Blind and Physically
    Handicapped
    Library of Congress
    Washington, DC 20542
    Established by an act of
    Congress in the 1930s, the
    National Library Service is a
    free national library program
    of braille and recorded
    materials for blind and
    physically handicapped
    persons. Books and
    magazines are selected and
    produced in braille and on
    recorded disk and cassette.
    Materials are distributed to a
    cooperating network of
    public libraries, where they
    are circulated to eligible
    borrowers. Reading
    materials and playback
    machines are sent to
    borrowers and returned to
    libraries by postage-free
    mail.
        Reference Circular No.
    93-3 is a comprehensive list
    of Bibles, Scriptures,
    liturgies, commentaries,
    concordances, and hymnals
    in special media which is
    available from the National
    Library Service. For further
    information: Check with
    your local library or contact
    the address above or on the
    Web: www.loc.gov.

Recording for the Blind &
    Dyslexic
    20 Roszel Rd.
    Princeton, NJ 08540
    Toll-free 1-800-221-4792
    Phone: (609) 452-0606
    Fax: (609) 520-7990

Providers of Alternative Media
Arizona

Sun Sounds
    Dede Pearse
    3124 East Roosevelt
    Phoenix, AZ 85008
    Phone: (602) 231-0500
    Braille, diskette, large print,
    audiocassette

California

AccuBraille
    Angela Desimoni
    30 Cleveland St.
    San Francisco, CA 94103
    Phone: (415) 863-8450
    Braille signs

The Braille Institute
    Carol Jimenez
    741 North Vermont Ave.
    Los Angeles, CA 90029-3594
    Phone: (213) 663-1111
    Braille

Flash Trans Enterprises
    4536 Edison Ave.
    Sacramento, CA 95821
    Phone: (916) 489-5860
    Fax: (916) 482-2250
    Audiotape/regular and both
    2- and 4-track cassette

Tom Karnes
    4529 18th St
    San Francisco, CA 94114-183111
    Phone: (415) 431-0245
    E-mail: Karnes@Net.com
    Braille, large print, diskette,
    and audiocassette

MSMT, Inc
    Carolyn Colclough
    West Barham Ave.
    Santa Rose, CA 95407
    Phone: (707) 579-1115
    Fax:(707) 579-1246
    Braille

Additional Resources

Connecticut

Transcription Technologies, Inc.
Marie Caputo
470 Tunnel Rd.
Vernon, CT 06066
Phone: (860) 643-1234
E-mail:
snuggles@sunspot.tiac.net
Braille, large-print,
audiocassette

Florida

Braille International, Inc.
3290 Southeast Slater St.
Stuart, FL 34997
Phone: (407) 286-8366
Fax: (407) 286-8909
Braille

Magnetix
Jim Baker
770 West Bay St.
Winter Garden, FL 34787
Phone: (407) 656-4494
Audiotape recording and
duplication

Illinois

Braille Line, Inc.
3901 North Vincent Ave.
Peoria Heights, IL 61614
Phone: (309) 686-0855
Braille

Guild for the Blind
180 North Michigan Ave.,
Suite 1700
Chicago, IL 60601
Phone: (312) 236-8569
Fax: (312) 236-8128
Braille

Naperville Area Transcribing
for the Blind (NATB)
Beverly Pfister
670 North Eagle St.
Naperville, IL 60563
(708) 963-0944

Kansas

Brick Barn Recording Studio
P.O. Box 414
Newton, KS 67114-0414
Phone: (888) 275-2276
E-mail: www.brickbarn.com
Audiotape recording and
duplication

The Dotted Line
Cindy Hallenbeck
1022 Jana Drive
Lawrence, KS 66049-3011
Phone: (913) 843-8700
E-mail: cindyh@idir.net

Kentucky

Recording for the Blind
Department
American Printing House
for the Blind
Contract Administration
1839 Frankfort Ave.
Louisville, KY 40206
Phone: (502) 895-2405
E-mail: APH@info.org
Audiotape. They can produce
materials on 4-track audiotape
in limited quantities (less than
500 copies).

Rick Roderick
2215 Westridge Rd.
Louisville, KY 40242
Phone:
(502) 423-8195 (home)
(502) 327-6010 (work)
E-mail: richard@iglou.com;
rick.roderick.parti@pcusa.org
Braille

Louisiana

Louisiana Center for the Blind
Zena Pearcy
101 South Trenton
Ruston, LA 71270
Phone: (318) 251-2891
Braille

Maine

Perspectives Total Accessibility
Specialists
15 May Street
Portland, ME 04102
Phone: (207) 772-7305
Braille

Maryland

Cutting Corporation
Mary Cutting
4940 Hampden Lane,
Ste. 300
Bethesda, MD 20814
Phone: (301) 654-2887
Audiotape recording and
duplication

Massachusetts

Braille Inc.
184 Seapit Rd.
East Falmouth, MA 02536-
0457
Phone: (508) 540-0800
Braille

Braille Production Program
Matthew Chao
Bay State Correctional
Center
P.O. Box 73
Norfolk, MA 02056
Phone: (617) 727-5046, ext.
171
Braille

Howe Press
Perkins School for the Blind
175 North Beacon St.
Watertown, MA 02172-2790
Phone: (617) 924-3434
Braille

Massachusetts Association
for the Blind
Attn: Braille Department
200 Ivy St.
Brookline, MA 02146
Phone: (617) 732-0249
Braille

National Braille Press
88 Saint Stephen St.
Boston, MA 02115
Phone: (617) 266-6061
Braille

Michigan

Michigan Braille Transcribing
Services
Fran Wonders
Jackson Prison
4000 Cooper St.
Jackson, MI 49201
Phone: (517) 780-6682
Braille

Minnesota

Volunteer Braille Services, Inc.
3730 Toledo Ave., North
Robbinsdale, MN 55422
Phone: (612) 521-0372
Braille

Additional Resources

Nebraska

Prose-Cons Braille
P.O. Box 2500
14th and Pioneer Blvds.
Lincoln, NE 68542-2500
Phone: (402) 471-3161
Braille

Nevada

Northern Nevada Braille
Transcribers
1015 Oxford Ave.
Sparks, NV 89431
Phone: (702) 358-2456
Braille

New York

Braille & Tactile Graphics
169 Kinglsley Rd.
Burnt Hills, NY 12027
Phone: (518) 399-7244
E-mail: rggately@aol.com
Braille

The First Baptist Church Braille
Service
64 Poplar Drive
Rochester, NY 14625
Phone: (716) 381-2127
E-mail:
JoAnnWiebeld@mlsonline.com
Braille

The Light House
111 East 59th St.
New York, NY 10022
Phone: (212) 821-9200
Braille

National Braille Association, Inc
3 Townline Circle
Rochester, NY 14623-2537
Phone: (716) 472-8260
Braille

North Carolina

Metrolina Association for the
Blind
704 Louise Ave.
Charlotte, NC 28204
(704) 372-3870
Braille

Ohio

Cleveland Sight Center
1909 East 101st St.
Cleveland, OH 44106
Phone: (216) 791-8118
Braille

Clovernook Center
7000 Hamilton Ave.
Cincinnati, OH 45231
Phone: (513) 522-3860
Braille

Pennsylvania

Dancing Dots Braille Music
Technology
130 Hampden Rd., 3rd floor
Upper Darby, PA 19082-
3110
Phone: (610) 352-7607
E-mail: ddots@netaxs.com
Braille

Bower Hill Braillists
70 Moffett St.
Pittsburgh, PA 15243
Phone: (512) 561-4114
Braille

Texas

Friendly Productions
3045 Lackland Rd., Ste. 210
Forth Worth, TX 76116
Phone: (817) 731-5908
Braille

Third Coast Braille Services
142 Lost Spring Drive
Floresville, TX 78114-9319
Phone: (210) 416-6138
E-mail: let216@juno.com
Braille

Washington

Blind Sight Braille Transcribing
14396 30th Ave. NE, Ste.
105
Seattle, WA 98125
Phone: (888) 278-5389
E-mail:
blndsite@baker.cnw.com
Braille

Northwest Braille Services
P.O. Box 234
Ferndale, WA 98248
Phone: (206) 733-6714
Braille

Services and Organizations Related to Deaf/Hard of Hearing/Speech

Alexander Graham Bell
Association for the Deaf
3417 Volta Place, NW
Washington, DC 20910-4500
Phone: (202) 337-5220
(Voice/TTY)

American Association of Deaf-
Blind (AADB)
814 Thayer Ave.
Silver Spring, MD 20910
Phone: (301) 588-6545
(Voice/TTY)

American Speech-Language-
Hearing Association
10801 Rockville Pike
Rockville, MD 20852
Toll-free: 1-800-638-8255
Fax: (301) 571-0457
E-mail: irc@asha.org

National Association of Black
Interpreters (NAOBI)
P.O. Box 70322
New Orleans, LA 70172-
0322

National Association of the
Deaf (NAD)
814 Thayer Ave.
Silver Spring, MD 20910
Phone: (301) 587-1788
TTY: (301) 587-1789

21

Additional Resources

Registry of Interpreters for the
Deaf, Inc. (RID)
8630 Fenton St.
Silver Spring, MD 20910
Phone: (301) 608-0050
(Voice/TTY)

Captioning Services

The Caption Center
125 Western Ave.
Boston, MA 02134
Phone: (617) 492-9255
Fax: (617) 562-0590

National Captioning Institute
5203 Leesburg Pike
Falls Church, VA 22041
Phone: (703) 998-2400

Assistive Listening Devices and Systems

National Information Center
on Deafness
Gallaudet University
Washington, DC 20002
Phone: (202) 651-5051
TDD: (202) 651-5052

Self-Help for Hard of Hearing
People (SHHH)
7800 Wisconsin Ave.
Bethesda, MD 20814
Phone: (301) 657-2248
TDD: (301) 657-2249

Learning Disabilities

Children and Adults with
Attention Deficit Disorder
(CH.A.D.D.)
499 N.W. 70th Ave., Ste. 308
Plantation, FL 38817
Phone: (954) 587-3700
Toll-free: 1-800-233-4050

International Dyslexia
Association
Chester Building
8600 LaSalle Rd., Ste. 382
Baltimore, MD 21286-2044
Phone: (410) 296-0232
Toll-free: 1-800-222-3123
E-mail: info@interdys.org

Learning Disabilities
Association of America (LDA)
4156 Library Rd.
Pittsburgh, PA 15234
Phone: (412) 341-1515
Fax: (412) 344-0224

National Center for Learning
Disabilities (NCLD)
381 Park Ave. South, Ste. 1420
New York, NY 10016
Phone: (212) 545-7510
Fax: (212) 545-9665
Toll-free Information &
Referral Service:
1-888-575-7373

Other

Bethesda Lutheran Homes and
Services, Inc.
700 Hoffmann Drive
Watertown, WI 53094
Phone: (414) 261-3050
A packet of materials for
planning worship with
persons with mental
retardation; includes
*Communion for Christians
Who are Mentally Retarded,*
a bibliography and
resources published
primarily by the Lutheran
Church.

Christian Literature
International
"New Life Publications
Catalogue"
P.O. Box 777
Canby, OR 97013
Simplified Bibles,
testaments, and teachers'
aids are available. These
publications use a simplified
vocabulary and substitute
easy-to-understand phrases
for difficult biblical words.

CRC Publications
2850 Kalamazoo Ave., SE
Grand Rapids, MI
49560-0001
1-800-333-8300
Phone: (616) 246-0834
Fax: 616-246-0834
Friendship—church
education curriculum for
people with mental
impairments—a three-year
curriculum that offers thirty
lessons per year at two
levels: youth and adult. The
curriculum goal is to aid
persons with mental
impairments to grow in and
profess their faith.

Eastern Christian Children's
Retreat
Chaplain Margot Hausmann
700 Mountain Ave.
Wyckoff, NJ 07481
To receive an updated list
including new suggestions
for *Multisensory Worship
Ideas,* send a self-addressed
stamped envelope to the
above address.

Robbinspring Publications
P.O. Box 13
Iron River, MI 49935
Toll-free: 1-800-507-2665
Several titles are available
for children, which promote
American Sign Language
translation, French and
Spanish, as well as English.
*Awful Abigail and Why She
Changed* is a Christmas
story about a little girl
whose parents run the inn
where Mary and Joseph
stayed when Jesus was
born.

3

Recognizing the Gifts of Persons with Developmental Disabilities, Mental Retardation, Mental Illness, and Other Brain-based Illnesses

" "

Our daughter Erin is fourteen years old. In addition to having Down syndrome, she has in the past two years developed a variety of physical problems, including recurring strokes. Our family was invited to attend our church when Erin was two years old by Erin's special education teacher, who was a member of the church. Her teacher was supportive of providing a Sunday school experience for Erin along with other children her age who did not have disabilities. So welcomed were we that we became members of this congregation. When she was younger, Erin used to proudly exclaim whenever we drove past the church throughout the week, "That's my church!"

—Beverly A. Wesche,
member of United Church,
Big Rapids, Michigan

" "

People with developmental disabilities have lifelong disabling conditions, which occurred at or before birth, in childhood or before the age of twenty-two. The conditions include mental retardation, spinal cord injury, epilepsy, sensory impairment, cerebral palsy, autism, and traumatic brain injury, as well as other conditions resulting in limitations. This legal definition of developmental disability dictates who may or may not be served by certain government programs.

The term "developmental disability" is complicated by the fact that some people with cerebral palsy, autism, or traumatic brain injury may have advanced intellectual skills but limited speech or physical function, while people with mental retardation have slower rates of learning and limited capacity for abstract thinking.[1]

A Place Called Acceptance*

Who among us does not long for a place that is safe—a place where we can take off our masks, be wholly ourselves, and still be accepted? Each of us longs for the unconditional love of Jesus Christ. The church, as the body of Christ, is the one place within this world we hope to find this kind of love and acceptance. The church is one place we trust we will be treated with dignity and respect, regardless of our gender, race, nationality, physical attributes, or mental capabilities.

What do parents of children with disabilities desire from their church communities? Parents of children with special needs long for a church where their children are loved and accepted just as they are. We live in a culture that worships physical beauty and judges a person's worth on what he or she produces or achieves. Our society often relegates persons with disabilities to a second-class citizenship, treating them with

*This information, reprinted from *A Place Called Acceptance: Ministry with Families of Children with Disabilities* (Louisville: Bridge Resources, 1999) by Kathleen Deyer Bolduc, is not intended to be disability specific. However, it is appropriate to children and adults with developmental disabilities and mental retardation. Bolduc writes both from the point of view of a professional and as a parent of a child with moderate mental retardation. Kathleen Deyer Bolduc, M.A., has researched and written extensively on disability's effect on the family system. She is married and the mother of three sons, the youngest of whom has mental retardation. Her manuscript titled *His Name is Joel: Searching for God in a Son's Disability* is being considered for publication, and she is working on a book of poetry with a theme of brokenness and wholeness. Kathy is a member of College Hill Presbyterian Church in Cincinnati, Ohio.

fear, pity, or condescension. Parents of children with disabilities long for a church that loves and accepts their children regardless of their appearance, behavior, or ability to achieve.

Unfortunately, children with disabilities and their families are not always lovingly enfolded into the arms of our churches. The mother of a child with both physical and mental disabilities writes, "We never found a church where we felt comfortable as fully participating members—each to his or her own capabilities." A frustrated mother of a young child with multiple disabilities writes, "Be accepting of our family and children as we are! God is, so why can't (you)? Understand that we have some very real limitations over which we have no control!" Another parent writes of her frustration at her congregation's lack of acceptance of her son's limitations due to his disability:

Most were not (accepting) of our son's "outbursts" during the services—he generally will sit very quietly, but if the room is very quiet (usually during silent prayer) he will let out one of his little whoops. I know it can be distracting, but far less distracting than a baby crying, as it only lasts a fraction of a second.

Parents whose children have physical or mental disabilities have the same needs for worship as any other member of a congregation, perhaps even more so, as they face an ongoing struggle that daily calls on physical, emotional, and spiritual reserves. Those whose children use wheelchairs must first be able to enter the sanctuary, however, before they can worship with the rest of the church community. Once within the building, they must be able to maneuver their way around the church facilities. When asked what her "dream church" looked

LYDIA GANS

    DIFFERENT MEMBERS, ONE BODY

like, the mother of a fifteen-year-old with multiple handicaps writes, "It would have ramps instead of stairs or back entrances. The bathrooms would be larger to care for personal needs."

Worship as community is foundational to the Christian life, regardless of family circumstances. Families that live with disability have the same needs for corporate prayer, praise, and hearing of the Word as any family. However, parents of children with special needs usually do not have the easy access to child care taken for granted by parents of typical children. Unless the church staff is willing to accommodate the special needs of each child, these parents lose the blessing of worship together as husband and wife, or as an entire family unit. One father wrote of the way his church handled a family's request to include their son, who had Down syndrome, into the Sunday school program, as recalled here:

> They were told their son couldn't be part of the class unless a parent was present all the time, which showed an appalling lack of desire to learn how to include this boy as well as no appreciation for those parents' need to worship together with other adults occasionally.

Raising a child with a disability is hard work. Parenthood is perhaps the hardest job any of us will undertake, and disability makes it even more difficult. The pressures of constant doctor and therapy visits, advocating for the child's rights in school, constant involvement with IEP teams (a team for an Individual Education Plan often involves as many as ten people), dealing with daily care at home, handling difficult behaviors—these kinds of caretaking necessities make this job stressful for any parent, regardless of income, education, strength of character, or depth of faith. Parents of children with special needs look to their church communities for prayer support, help with child care, occasional meals, assistance with transportation when schedules become overwhelming, offers to include their special children in various church events, listening ears, shoulders to cry on, and support groups with whom they can share struggles and joys. They especially appreciate support from pastors and church staff in the form of counseling and occasional phone calls to see how they are doing.

Parents of children with disabilities want their children to have the opportunity to attend Sunday school with peers. This will undoubtedly mean that some type of accommodation will have to be made. Most parents of children with unique learning challenges long for a church where the Christian education staff will welcome their children as well as accommodate them in whatever way is necessary, without the parents having to do all the work.

The prevailing cultural view is one that says people with disabilities are *to be served;* are incapable of giving back to the community. Parents of children who are physically or mentally challenged look to the church community to help discern and use their child's unique nature and gifts. A mother whose young son has moderate mental retardation writes,

> I want the church members to take more of a responsibility in my son's upbringing, as in the philosophy "It takes a whole village to raise a child." I would want my child to feel that our church family was a place where he was safe, loved, and respected for his contribution.

Parents of children with disabilities, like any parents, desire that their children's lives be filled with friends. Because inclusion is the exception rather than the norm in our schools and communities, parents of special children dream that their church community might be one place their children will experience the joys of friendship. Some parents feel stigmatized and different because of their child's disability. They too desire friendships within the church. They especially desire the friendship of other families with whom they can socialize and celebrate and receive the extra support they might need.

A father expresses his belief that friendships between disabled and nondisabled children benefits both:

> Some of the research on inclusion . . . shows that children without disabilities show greater compassion, less stereotypes, and even less fears about failure when in classrooms with children with disabilities. What better way to develop evangelical entrepreneurs than to have children learning from each other about perseverance, alternative methods of learning, and even coping with failure?

What Can My Church Do to Welcome Children with Disabilities and Their Families?*

Greet the child with a disability in the same way you would greet any other child. Although she may be incapable of responding in typical fashion, she will feel welcomed by your greeting. Talk directly to the child rather than using the child's parent as a translator. If the child does not answer immediately, be patient. Get down on the child's level and establish eye contact. Repeat your statement or question, if necessary. If the child responds and you cannot understand what he says, ask him to repeat himself. Even if the conversation ends up going nowhere, you have still communicated to the child that he is important in your eyes.

Fear of unpredictable behaviors often keeps church members from reaching out with compassion to those who are disabled. Behavioral issues are fairly common with some disabilities, such as autism, attention deficit disorder, and mental retardation. Try to understand that the behavior is part of the disability, not a character flaw. When a child with a disability behaves inappropriately, use as little "fanfare" as possible in your response. The more attention you pay to the behavior, the more you reinforce the very behavior you do not want. Attempt to redirect the child, changing activities if necessary. Common sense goes a long way in most instances. Treat the child lovingly yet firmly, respect boundaries of personal space, avoid situations that are known to upset the child. Ask the child's parents what techniques they use in handling disruptive behaviors.

Allow the child to do as much for herself as possible. Sometimes it will take the child longer to complete a certain task. Be patient. Be there to give assistance, but do not impose yourself unless needed. Find ways the child can contribute in Sunday school or within the context of worship. Perhaps she can help pass out bulletins, be responsible for getting the pastor a drink of water before the service, help pass out papers in Sunday school, or clean up after class. Children with disabilities like to feel needed, just as all children do. Use a multisensory teaching approach when teaching children with disabilities. *All* children will benefit from a lesson that uses all five senses.

Encourage families with challenged children to take part in all areas of congregational life. Issue a special invitation to church picnics, retreats, potluck dinners, for example. Offer to help out with transportation or with a "big buddy" for a child whose disability makes relaxation for her parents difficult. Many people, when confronted by children who are physically or mentally "different," choose to remain in their comfort zone by using avoidance behavior. This sends a strong message . . . one that says, "I don't care enough to want to get to know you." Others, wanting to reach out, don't know what to say or do. A simple "Hi! How are you today?" is a simple enough place to begin and makes child and family feel welcome. If you notice a family member struggling with a child, either behaviorally or perhaps in getting a wheelchair in or out of a car, don't be afraid to ask if there is anything you can do to help.

Some people mistakenly believe you must have special training to work with children with disabilities. While training would be a bonus, this simply isn't true. All that is truly necessary is an open, nonjudgmental attitude, patience, a love for children, and a desire to share the gospel of Jesus Christ. Consider holding workshops on disability issues on an occasional basis. Ask parents of children with special needs for input, or perhaps to lead a class to educate the congregation in how to reach out to those who are disabled. Use "people-first" language when talking about disabilities.

Keep the families who are struggling with disability on your church prayer list for intercessory prayer. Prayer support is one of the greatest gifts a congregation can give to these families. Be sure to let the families know you are praying for them.

*Kathleen Deyer Bolduc, *A Place Called Acceptance: Ministry with Families of Children with Disabilities* (Louisville: Bridge Resources, 1999). Reprinted and edited with permission.

Mental Illness and Other Brain-based Illnesses

❝ ❞

Find ways to speak to my health and strength, rather than focusing on my mental illness.

—Nancy Lee Head,
member of the Church of the Pilgrims,
Washington, D.C.

❝ ❞

A person with a mental illness has a biological dysfunction in his or her brain that may cause serious disturbances in the way the person thinks, feels, and relates to other people. Because of the disorder, the person may find it difficult to cope with the ordinary demands of daily life. Such disorders affect individuals of all ages, and they occur in many American families, across all boundaries of income, education, race, and ethnicity.

The exact causes of the many severe mental illnesses, sometimes called psychiatric disorders, are not known. These are brain-based illnesses that are not caused by poor parenting or other social causes. They are treatable illnesses. With appropriate medical care, a person with a mental illness can lead a life of quality.[2]

The National Institute of Mental Health (NIMH) says that today in America thirty-five million people suffer from some form of mental illness and that one in four of American families is affected. Mental illness is twice as prevalent as Alzheimer's disease, six times as prevalent as diabetes, and five times as prevalent as multiple sclerosis. More American hospital beds are occupied by people who have a mental illness than by those who have cancer, heart, and lung disease combined.[3] Yet, this is a disability that may carry with it a greater stigma than any other disability. As a faith community, our fears often prevent us from reaching out to persons with a mental illness. We are afraid of saying the wrong thing or we are just afraid. Being in community with a person who has a mental illness and with the person's family requires a loving commitment of time and perhaps long-term emotional support and ongoing encouragement.

It requires that we build a relationship based on mutual friendship and respect and not one in which we act like a therapist or other person in authority. A person who has a mental illness that is periodic or episodic in nature needs the same from us as any other person who has a disability: cards and flowers and phone calls when hospitalization is needed, assistance with meals and transportation, and of course prayers.

Before I Started to Serve*

When we think of disability, we imagine a person who uses a wheelchair or a cane, or being led by a Seeing Eye dog or communicating with sign language. But many disabilities, although just as severe, are less readily apparent. Mental disabilities are in this category. I have suffered from mental illness, and at times have been incapacitated by it; but, generally, I appear normal. My illness, schizophrenia, does not involve split or multiple personalities, as the general public believes. This is a misconception fueled by the mass media and Hollywood movies. Schizophrenia is an umbrella word for many kinds of symptoms, some of which are the following: thought disorder, hallucinations (auditory or visual), delusions, apathy, and withdrawal. A person may have some or all of these; individual cases vary enormously. Medication is often used to control most or all of these symptoms, with much success.

Some Christians believe that a person need only have a healthy relationship with God to get free of mental illness. Pastors and churches with this belief condemn and ostracize the mentally ill, stating they are to blame for their disease. The causes of mental illness are complex, but include biological, as well as psychological and environmental, factors. Any of these factors or a combination may damage a person, causing severe emotional disorder. I believe some Christian people have a view of severe mental illness that is misinformed. Their harsh judgment of those of us with psychiatric disabilities impedes our recovery and may cause a crisis of faith. In my home church and

*Marcia A. Murphy is a freelance writer and volunteer editor of the *Outback Press*, the newsletter of the Outback Clubhouse, a rehabilitation center in Iowa City, Iowa.

Bible study group there is an environment that fosters acceptance of those of us who have mental and emotional difficulties.

In 1994, I began attending St. Andrew Presbyterian Church, three blocks from my home. Before I started to serve in various ways there, I requested a Stephen minister. The pew card said, "Need a friend?" And, since I did, I filled out the card. The Stephen minister made weekly visits to my home and became a friend I could talk to about religious matters. We had a lot in common, as her daughter had schizophrenia. When I had questions pertaining to spiritual issues, she encouraged me to meet with the pastor. He became very helpful. He had experience counseling persons with mental illness and knew about schizophrenia.

The compassion of the Stephen minister and the pastor gave hope that perhaps I had found a community of believers that would accept me. The secular world stigmatizes those of us with psychiatric disabilities; therefore, I had felt degraded and unworthy. When these church members treated me respectfully, I began to gain a sense of dignity. I began volunteering at the church by participating in the prayer ministry. The coordinator welcomed me with open arms. Eventually, I shared with her that I had a psychiatric disability, but she continued to be friendly and appreciative of my involvement in the group. I wrote a small article on the prayer ministry for the church newsletter at her request. We had lunch together and got to know each other more deeply. However, after a while, I found this ministry too difficult, and withdrew from it.

The senior pastor then suggested that I attend an ecumenical women's Bible study that met in my church. This group has been a major healing force for me. After I had attended for a month, I volunteered to prepare coffee and set up the chairs. At first, I was extremely anxious and frightened about the commitment. Learning the task was a challenge. There were times I called the group leader to say I was unable to help that week. Then she would find a substitute, but this happened infrequently. One member, who confided to me that she had bipolar (manic-depressive) disorder, offered to take my place if I felt unable to set up. She also is the person who encouraged me to join the church (I had been attending only as a visitor). Now, I have attended the Bible study three-and-

NANCY ANNE DAWE

a-half years and no longer have trouble with the preparation. I am confident that I will not fail. I increased my involvement by working in the kitchen when there were potlucks. Also, when memorial services with luncheons were held for members of the group at my church, I was asked to bake cookies and to help serve. Once, when there was a potluck, a group member phoned to invite me (for I had missed the weekly meeting). She said, "You don't have to bring anything. Just bring yourself." Her friendship has been steadfast, and she has tried to learn more about my illness. Also, she has sent many greeting cards for various holidays.

The atmosphere of respect and trust at St. Andrew has allowed me to feel comfortable enough to volunteer in a number of ways. I have collated the monthly newsletters and the annual reports. I have served coffee between services before the adult education class—I was, at first, self-conscious and afraid of interacting so closely with the congregation as I poured coffee. After doing this several times, however, I grew accustomed to the task and enjoyed it. A friend asked me to be a greeter with her at worship services. I found this rewarding and I enjoyed shaking hands with dozens of members.

I have described numerous ways in which the church has encouraged me, a person with psychiatric disabilities, to be involved. It has been merciful, as Jesus would be. When the powerful and destructive force of stigmatization breaks the hearts of the mentally ill, the church, as an instrument of God's love, helps them to find fellowship and restoration of human dignity.

✔✔✔

What Can My Church Do to Nurture the Gifts of Persons with Mental Illness?

An Interview with Nancy Lee Head*

For Nancy Lee Head, the act of serving dinner to homeless women at a shelter is as holy an act as serving Communion to a congregation would be for an ordained minister. Washing the lice off another resident's back is as sacred an act as baptizing a child would be for an ordained pastor. Nancy says, "Reinterpreting these two sacraments of the Presbyterian Church (U.S.A.) became very important to me when I was rejected as a candidate for the ordained ministry by that same denomination in 1978 because I had been diagnosed with schizophrenia some eighteen years before."

Nancy says that her prayers during the early years of struggle with schizophrenia were "simple and stark: God, I am so scared. God, I know you did not create me to end like this. God, please keep me from getting bitter during this difficult time. Please help me to learn from this awful experience, and if I live through it, help me to be softer and more vulnerable to others who have suffered and are suffering in a similar situation."

These days, Nancy believes that the gift of faith and her spirituality have been enriched by mental illness and vice versa. She has learned to manage her illness, and although she is humble in the knowledge that she is on a day-by-day journey, she sheds some light on learning to live a faith-filled life with serious mental illness and shares these points:

Personal boundaries, "where I begin as a

> ON THE DAY
> I CALLED, YOU
> ANSWERED ME,
> YOU INCREASED
> MY STRENGTH
> OF SOUL.
>
> —Ps. 138:3

person and end and where the rest of the world begins and ends," are often a problem for some persons with schizophrenia and other types of mental illnesses. When this situation occurs in the extreme, it can cause extreme fear and disorientation, a sense of loss of self. "I have learned that I have to have a place and time where, as the late writer May Sarton stated, 'I come back into myself.' I do this through silence or music or meditation—to remain centered in God, the Ground of my being."

Nancy suggests that her church community helps most by finding ways to speak to her health and strength, rather than focusing on her mental illness. During a hospitalization, two women from her church visited, bringing a box of greeting cards and a book of stamps. They had remembered that one of Nancy's ministries is sending cards to members of the congregation who might need cheering up or for important occasions. This simple, loving act by these women from her church was an important witness to God's love. Another time, Nancy had volunteered to make cookies for an event but was later too ill to manage that task. With help, she was still able to contribute by placing the dough on a cookie sheet. Other small acts like these are very meaningful to persons with mental illness who want and need to continue being part of the church and who can still contribute even when they are ill.

*Nancy Lee Head has served the Presbyterian Church (U.S.A.) as a lay employee in a variety of positions for over thirty years. Since 1991, she has been program director for the Alliance for the Mentally Ill—D.C., and has helped to organize the D.C., Consumers League. Comments are excerpted from an article that originally appeared as "My Life as Ministry: Unusually Connected with Other People," *The Journal*, published by the California Alliance for the Mentally Ill, Vol. 8, No. 4 (1997).

Additional Resources

Mental Retardation, Developmental Disabilities

The Religion Division, American Association on Mental Retardation (AAMR), is an interdenominational resource sharing group that provides a number of resources, including a bibliography of resources for clergy, laypersons, families, and service providers. The 1998 edition, *Dimensions of Faith and Congregational Ministries with Persons with Developmental Disabilities and Their Families*, is available for $10 (prepaid) from: Religion Division, AAMR, 31 Alexander St., Princeton, NJ 08540.

The National Clearinghouse on Managed Care and Long-Term Services and Supports for Adults with Developmental Disabilities and Their Families—www.mcare.net

American Association on Mental Retardation
444 North Capitol St., NW, Ste. 846
Washington, D.C. 20001-1512
Phone : (202) 387-1968
Toll-free: 1-800-424-3688
Fax: (202) 387-2193
E-mail: info@aamr.org; www.aamr.org

The Association of Retarded Citizens (ARC) of the United States
500 East Border St., Ste. 300
Arlington, TX 76010
Phone: (817) 261-6003
Fax: (817) 277-3491
TDD: (817) 277-0553
E-mail: thearc@metronet.com

National Association of Developmental Disabilities Councils
1234 Massachusetts Ave., NW, Suite 103
Washington, DC 20005
Phone: (202) 347-1234
Fax: (202) 347-4023
E-mail: www.igc.apc.org/NADDC

Speaking for Ourselves
One Plymouth Meeting, Ste. 630
Plymouth Meeting, PA 19462
Phone: (610) 825-4592
Fax: (610) 825-4595
E-mail: speakingfo@aol.com

Mental Illness and Other Brain-based Disabilities

National Alliance for the Mentally Ill (NAMI) is an organization that provides advocacy, research regarding the availability of services, educational efforts, and a toll-free helpline (1-800-950-6264) for persons seeking information about mental illness. The mailing address is NAMI, 200 North Gleeb Rd., Ste. 1015, Arlington, VA 22203. The Web address is: www.NAMI.org. *The Journal*, available by subscription, is timely, balanced, and highly readable with each issue on one aspect of mental illness. $25 per year. California Alliance for the Mentally Ill (C.A.M.I.), 1111 Howe Ave., Ste. 475, Sacramento, CA 95825. Phone: 916-567-0163.

National Mental Health Services, Knowledge Exchange Network (KEN) was developed by the Center for Mental Health Services (CMHS) for users of mental health services and their families; the general public; policymakers; the media; and those who design, finance, and provide mental health services. KEN is a national, one-stop source of information and resources on prevention, treatment, and rehabilitation services for mental illness. KEN's toll-free telephone service is available Monday through Friday from 8:30 A.M. to 5:00 P.M., EST, at 1-800-789-CMHS. Telecommunication Device for the Deaf (TDD) service is available to users at (301) 443-9006. KEN's World Wide Web address is http://www.mentalhealth.org; e-mail: ken@mentalhealth.org.

4

Including Persons with Hidden Disabilities

❝ ❞

For those who simply can no longer attend services, Westminster provides a tape ministry. Lil records the church service each Sunday. Although he is legally blind, Randy makes copies of the tapes. The deacon of the week delivers the tapes, which provide (members) with a way of staying connected to the life of the church.

—Edith Edson, member of
Westminster Presbyterian Church,
Pueblo, Colorado

❝ ❞

(A hidden disability is a condition that may) persist for months or years and generally interferes with an individual's everyday ability to function. The effects of the particular illness may be invisible or can be camouflaged until the most acute state begins. Thus, few people in the congregation may know that the person is ill. For others, periodic "flare ups" may require hospitalization and result in some of the disabling conditions described elsewhere.[1]

Hidden disabilities (sometimes called invisible disabilities) include chronic illness, such as diabetes, lupus, arthritis, and AIDS/HIV; allergies, chronic fatigue syndrome, multiple chemical sensitivity, and other immune system disorders. Hidden disabilities also include such disorders as cancer, visual impairments, respiratory ailments, chronic psychiatric disorders, and gastrointestinal conditions. The cycle of relapses and remissions of many of

these disabling conditions make it difficult for members with these conditions to participate fully in the life of the congregation. Persons with such conditions are often afraid to talk about them because they do not want to appear weak or face possible rejection. In some cases these fears are valid, because other members of the congregation may not understand the condition and may be afraid of contracting it. In spite of these barriers, churches can and do offer ministries that welcome and cherish the lives of persons who have hidden disabilities.

Is She Really as Sick as She Says She Is?*

When June said, "I can't," it was because of her lupus, a progressive, destructive, painful, invisible illness. She looked fine, but we knew she was ill. One day at Bible study she said, "I once asked my doctor if he could just bandage me up for a while so people would know how bad I'm hurting." Through her I became aware of invisible disability, its devastating limitations, and the additional pain that unknowing church and community friends often inflict. Little did I know that, years later, I would be suffering an invisible disability called chronic fatigue syndrome (CFIDS) (Chronic Fatigue Immune Dysfunction Syndrome), be forced to resign from my life work as pastor, avoid community, and rarely be able to even attend worship.

Those who are suffering from what we call

---

*Kay Dawson Puckett is a Presbyterian pastor with a disability, sidelined on the farm in Ohio. This text first appeared in *PDC News* (May/June 1998). Used with permission.

hidden or invisible disability look like normal healthy people. "Is she really as sick as she says she is?" The question was about a member who had sung a sweet soprano solo the Sunday before. I knew she had saved up her strength to sing and would be bedfast for several days after that Herculean effort, for only half her heart was functional. But no one would see her then—at home following worship.

Spending a worship hour sitting in a pew, visiting with others, and joining in responses and hymns may provoke painful and sometimes life-threatening symptoms to those with invisible disability. To be unable to even participate in church gatherings adds another layer to the trauma of a hidden, debilitating illness.

As a pastor, I named such individuals to our "At Home Congregation" and asked them to be our praying corps when they couldn't get to worship. I know they made a difference.

Every congregation can, with a little planning, include persons with invisible disabilities:

- Mail the weekly bulletin to be in hand by Sunday worship.

- Recognize the "At Home Congregation" in worship. It may change week by week, just as the members of the congregation who are physically present do.

- Offer Communion at home, even though these parishioners are not fully "shut in."

- Make video- or audiotapes of worship available by mail or personal delivery.

- Respect energy limits, but recruit from this group to help out with telephoning, note writing, newspaper-clip files. Use their skills. One may do church bookkeeping at home, while another repairs items for the church garage sale.

- Be supportive through parish nurse or regular visitation programs, which usually only reach the fully shut-in.

- When considering persons with invisible disabilities, don't forget financial stewardship. When people are kept linked with their congregation, they often continue their financial support. A church I once served showed a marked decrease in contributions from the "shut-ins" when visitation was infrequent.

- Use new means of keeping in touch, such as the computer and on-line services. My own frustration being at home during worship led to the creation of a meeting called "Sunday Sidelined" on PresbyNet, the PC(USA)'s on-line service (see chapter 8). Here, sometime during the week, as many as fifty or sixty people read the Sunday lectionary lessons and a sermonette and may participate in a *cybereucharist*. I now feel part of the worship community, many with invisible disabilities. Tell your at-home congregation about PresbyNet. It's a great place to meet new friends when you're unable to attend worship.

Are some who no longer take their place in your pews suffering from an invisible disability? Welcoming all through accessibility features is the first step. Go one step farther. Identify and include those with invisible disability even if they are at home when the church bells ring.

The Jeremiah Project*

❝ ❞

Our church . . . formed a nonprofit corporation out of the session to minister to persons suffering from MCS (Multiple Chemical Sensitivity). We bought 1.5 acres of land, an old mobile home, dug a well and a septic system, brought in electricity and telephone, and are in the process of rebuilding the mobile home after stripping it to the walls and redesigning the interior. All of the rebuilding involves using safe building materials (that a person with MCS can tolerate).

—Richard S. Robertson, member of Westminster Presbyterian Church, Austin, Texas

❝ ❞

Nestled in the rolling hills of central Texas is the headquarters of a unique interdenominational

*Linda K. Reinhardt founded the Jeremiah Project in 1994 and is herself disabled as a result of pesticide poisoning. For more information about chemical injury or the Jeremiah Project, contact the ministry at 222 Soft Wind, Canyon Lake, TX 78133. This text is reprinted with permission by Access Press, 1821 University Ave., W., Ste. 185N, St. Paul, MN 55104.

ministry sponsored by the Presbyterian Church
(U.S.A.). The Jeremiah Project provides an open-
air worship center, a resource library, and
recreation areas, all free of pesticides,
fragrances, and other chemicals, for people who
have survived a chemical injury/poisoning. The
chemically injured can no longer participate in
the mainstream of life, including church, due to
the need to avoid further contact with even the
smallest amounts of everyday chemicals. A life
of suffering and isolation is the result of these
sensitivities and debilitating reactions.

The ministry also offers a variety of services
to over a thousand individuals nationwide who
are homebound and isolated by this devastating
condition, via an uplifting newsletter, audiotapes
of worship and Bible study, and over-the-
telephone pastoral care.

In addition, the Jeremiah Project has
created programs and curriculum for churches
and materials for individuals to help educate the
public about the overuse of pesticides and the
adverse health effects of synthetic fragrances,
solvents, and other personal care and
household products.

United States government agencies estimate
that 15 percent of the general population are
affected by these chemical products. Chemical
sensitivity is an invisible disability that cannot
be accommodated by usual means of
accessibility. The Jeremiah Project fill the void,
offering hope and encouragement to individuals
and families, while empowering churches to
reach out to those in their own community who
are chemically injured. The chemically injured
include: workers with sick building syndrome,
people with chronic fatigue, those poisoned
with pesticides, women with silicone breast
implants, Gulf War veterans, and children born
with hypersensitivity.

✔✔✔

What Can My Church Do to Live a Less Toxic Lifestyle?*

Begin a gradual transition of using less harmful products. You will soon discover how much you can do without. An additional bonus: You will save money.

1. Purchase and use unscented detergents. Avoid using fabric softeners, especially dryer sheets. (Scents are synthetic compounds that are irritants, neurotoxins, and carcinogens.)

2. Use safer flea control methods—herbal flea collars or prescribed flea neutralization (ask your veterinarian).

3. Throw away aerosol cans of Raid, Black Flag, Off, and other over-the-counter pesticides. There are a number of resources that are safer alternatives for bug control and repellant. Contact the Jeremiah Project for more details. Phone: (830) 935-4618; or write: 222 Soft Wind, Canyon Lake, TX 78133.

4. Ask your grocer to stock organic produce. Purchase organic produce when available. The cost may be higher now, but will come down as more people make this choice.

5. When purchasing new clothes, select 100 percent cotton or other natural fibers whenever possible. Also purchase only cotton or natural-fiber linens. Leave the synthetic petrochemicals and formaldehyde behind.

6. Choose unscented personal-care

> FOR SURELY I KNOW THE PLANS I HAVE FOR YOU, SAYS THE LORD, PLANS FOR YOUR WELFARE AND NOT FOR HARM, TO GIVE YOU A FUTURE WITH HOPE.
>
> —JER. 29:11

products: soaps, shampoos, deodorants, cosmetics, lotions, hair spray, mousses, gels, and so on. Each product is a chemical compound not regulated by EPA or FDA. The added fragrance includes up to 600 additional petrochemicals per product. These chemicals are skin and respiratory irritants, neurotoxic (affecting the central nervous system), and many are proven carcinogens.

7. If you must use pest control, switch to an Integrated Pest Management (IPM) system, which is the least toxic available. (For some sensitive people and asthmatics, IPM is not suitable.)

8. Use inexpensive, "homemade" cleaning products: white vinegar, baking soda, salt, and lemon juice are excellent choices. Contact the Jeremiah Project for more information.

9. Avoid wearing perfume in public places. You can do a great deal to lessen the load of pollution and improve indoor air quality at work, businesses, and church simply by not wearing fragrance. Your fragrance, like second-hand smoke, affects the health of those around you.

10. Make a commitment to be better informed. Read any two of the books on the Jeremiah Project reading/resource list in the next year.

*From a handout written by the Rev. Linda K. Reinhardt of the Jeremiah Project regarding multiple chemical sensitivity, an invisible disability thought to be triggered by exposure to pesticides or other petrochemicals. Reinhardt founded the Jeremiah Project in 1994 and is herself disabled as a result of pesticide poisoning.

Additional Resources

The Alchemy of Illness, by Kat Duff. New York: Bell Tower, an imprint of Harmony Books, 1993. A first-person account of a woman's spiritual journey with Chronic Fatigue Immune Dysfunction Syndrome.

The American Association for Chronic Fatigue Syndrome
c/o Harborview Medical Center
325 Ninth Ave., Box 359780
Seattle, WA 98104
Phone: (206) 521-1932
Fax: (206) 521-1930
E-mail: debrap@u.washington.edu

"Food for Thought," a program planner/ curriculum for churches. Suggested donation, $35. Videos and other materials are available. Contact: The Jeremiah Project, 222 Soft Wind, Canyon Lake, TX 78133.

Healthy Living in a Toxic World: Simple Ways to Protect Yourself and Your Family from Hidden Health Risks, by Cynthia Fincher, Ph.D. Colorado Springs, CO: Pinon Press, 1996.

Visit the Invisible Disabilities Page at www.shore.net/~dmoisan/invisible_disability

Westminster Environmental Illness Assistance, Inc., is a ministry of Westminster Presbyterian Church in Austin, Texas, that works in the area of multiple chemical sensitivity. Contact Richard S. Robertson, Westminster Environmental Illness Assistance, Inc., 3208 Exposition Blvd., Austin, TX 78703.

5

Removing Architectural Barriers

"

I first started attending this church because they had a ramp and it was so easy for me to get in the building. I did not need to depend on help from any member of my family, but could come alone if necessary.

—Helen Thompson,
twenty-year member of
Harvey Browne Presbyterian Church,
Louisville, Kentucky

"

A 1993 Presbyterian Panel survey found that a majority of respondents thought that inaccessible church facilities impeded involvement by persons with disabilities.[1] Churches that contributed their stories for this book have acknowledged this fact and have worked to find ways to make their churches more welcoming places. Regardless of the size of the congregation, the amount of financial resources, or location, they share several common threads of experience. Many reported that the elimination of attitudinal and perceptual barriers was an important first step in convincing others to make accommodations— and usually the most difficult. Once the attitudinal barriers were removed, all the other issues such as funding and design became less significant. Other churches observed that a single member functioned as a catalyst when he or a member of his family became disabled. Few, however, reported that their churches devised a strategy or long-term plan for making access a priority *without* education or intervention happening first. Many churches that

contributed information also said that funding access changes and renovations came from a combination of sources including low-interest loans available from the PCUSA,[2] designated giving, capital fund drives, special fund appeals, funds from estates designated for specific projects, and funds allocated in annual church budgets.

Where to Begin?

Edith Edson, a member of Westminster Presbyterian Church in Pueblo, Colorado, writes:

Like most congregations, Westminster did not intentionally discriminate, . . . they were simply not aware of the needs of folks who have disabling conditions. They needed to learn to see with fresh eyes. As they listened to members and friends, they began to make changes, most of them costing very little.

Westminster began thinking about access and inclusion in 1970, and Ms. Edson credits "farsighted individuals in the congregation" for seeing that there were no architectural barriers when the new sanctuary was built in that same year. The church installed movable pews of different lengths so that persons who used wheelchairs could have choices in where to sit and would not block the aisles. Granted, new church construction makes it easier to provide access, but Ms. Edson writes that in 1983 church members "realized that it was not enough for the building to be accessible; worship services needed to be accessible as well." They spent a couple of years investigating different types of assistive hearing devices and eventually purchased several. Large-print Bibles, hymnals, and bulletins were made available in subsequent years, along with the addition of more accessible parking areas.

Westminster's process of improving access was also a learning process for the congregation and leadership. "In the early 1980s, (Westminster) initiated a telephone dial-in system for Sunday morning worship. However, it was discontinued because of lack of use." This led to the discovery that audiotapes work better because listeners can use them at their convenience. Members record the service each Sunday, and the deacon of the week delivers the copies to those who need them. Other materials, such as the church newsletter, daily devotions, and choir music are made available on tape or enlarged as needed. Westminster has been open to change over the years, and Ms. Edson says, "As the church strives, with new vision, to seek solutions, they will undoubtedly discover ways to make worship and service more meaningful for all people who enter." Funding for all the access changes begun in 1970 until now has come from funds from an estate designated for such changes as the movable pews and from funds authorized by session.

Warminster Presbyterian Church in Warminster, Pennsylvania, has been accepting the access challenge since 1975, when one of its members had a stroke and wanted to continue to worship but had no way to get into the building. Calvin Uzelmeier, pastor of the church, says, "The session immediately voted to take money out of the budget and construct the ramp, even though we did not have any guidelines to follow. . . . Once we took that first step (construction of the ramp), everything else seemed to fall into place."

Over the past two decades, Warminster has gradually made a number of other changes. Bathrooms were made wheelchair accessible. When a deaf couple began attending worship, sign-language–interpreted services were held, first on special holidays, then on the first Sunday of the month, then twice a month, and now every week, with the cost for the signer now a part of the regular budget. When a family with a daughter who has retardation saw the ramp and heard the church was interested in disability, they began attending. Curriculum and Sunday school was changed to include this child, and soon more children with retardation began to attend. Large-print Bibles, hymnbooks, and Sunday morning bulletins, assistive hearing

devices, and disability awareness experiences have evolved over the years to become standard in Warminster's life. Subtle changes, such as repeating creeds and prayers slowly, combined with the visible architectural changes, has had an added benefit, according to Mr. Uzelmeier. "The congregation has become aware of God's invitation to *all* people."

Paul Rosenberger is a member of First Presbyterian Church in Decatur, Illinois. He has sung in the church choir since he joined the church in 1955. The choir sits each Sunday in an area that is on the second floor—perhaps a total of twenty-five steps. In 1983 Paul contracted Guillain-Barré syndrome and began using a wheelchair. In the following year, the session approved funds to purchase a platform chair lift to enable him to get to the choir area. In 1993, the three-story educational wing of the church was renovated to include two accessible bathrooms, an addition to house an elevator, and a new ramp to the balcony. "Even though I might have been the trigger for some of this, the elevator, and hence the church building, is now used by many elderly and disabled people who otherwise might stay away." Rosenberger says that the renovation for the education building was funded by a combination of a capital campaign project, designated giving, and special offerings.

Trinity Presbyterian Church in Scotia, New York, tackled the issue of barrier removal with a plan of action. Member Mariellen Boomhower chaired a committee at the church that is making the building more accessible. She began doing research on the project two years ago at the public library and says, "I thought it would be a lot easier to find information than it actually was. I was naive enough to think I could easily get grant funding too." Barrier removal included installing an accessible bathroom, a permanent ramp, and an updated sound system to enhance sound quality. Mariellen says, "It has been quite an accomplishment for our small-town church of about 130 members. I think the biggest challenge was helping the congregation become aware that there was a need for this." Helping the congregation to look at inclusion differently happened gradually and was facilitated by sermons, appeals by Ms. Boomhower, the formation of an accessibility committee, and a four-week program, which included members of the congregation who either had a disability or knew someone with a disability.

After the congregation was able to see the benefits of making access changes, they enthusiastically embraced the project. Funding, however, did not come easily to this small congregation. Ms. Boomhower says that initial funding came when a member of the church died and the session voted to set the memorial money aside as seed money. "We also patched together money from our small budget surplus. We finally asked each family to donate $150 toward the project."

Crescent Hill Presbyterian Church in Louisville, Kentucky, dedicated its newly renovated and accessible sanctuary on World Communion Sunday in 1997. Like Trinity Presbyterian Church, Crescent Hill's journey involved several stages of a growing understanding about welcoming persons with disability. Careful planning, study, reflection, and prayer that involved the entire 230-member congregation over a number of years resulted in a capital campaign and pledge drive in 1996. The church now has an entryway that is accessible at the front of the sanctuary, accessible rest rooms, pew cuts for wheelchairs, improved lighting, and a brighter sanctuary.

Crescent Hill Presbyterian Church

Universal Design

When beginning to think about the idea of removing physical barriers to accommodate persons with disabilities, think "universal access," or barrier removal that will benefit the greatest number of people whether they have a disability or not. This means putting aside momentarily what we know about the legal minimum requirements when making access changes, to think about what is needed to enable the greatest number of persons whether they hear or not, whether they speak or not. *Universal Design* depends on "designing buildings and products so they can be used by everyone."[3] Rocker switches in rooms are easy to use for persons who don't have disabilities, but they are often the only means of accessing light for some persons with disabilities. Ramps are critical to a person in a wheelchair who wants to enter a building. Ramps, are not the best way to enter a building, however, for persons with other disabilities. Walking up an incline may cause some persons pain and instability to hip and knee joints, which could result in a fall. For persons with these kinds of disabilities, stairs may prove best. Using the principle of universal design, the best way to accommodate the greatest number of persons is to build neither ramp nor stairs, but to have an entryway that is level with the street. Two tiny bathrooms, one for women and one for men, could be combined into one larger bathroom that is large enough for a wheelchair user to navigate or a parent with a child in a stroller. A standard-height water fountain can be used by a person in a wheelchair or a child or short-statured person if a paper-cup dispenser is mounted near the fountain. Latch door handles can be operated easily by a person with limited mobility or a person with a stack of hymnals in her hand—these are all examples of the universal design concept.

People with Disabilities Explain It All for You: Your Guide to the Public Accommodations Requirements of the Americans with Disabilities Act outlines a few basic principles for universal design that can be utilized in making our churches more inviting:

1. Don't think "special." Special means separate and different. It means "segregated.". . . People with disabilities don't like coming in the back door by the loading dock or having to use separate restrooms and water fountains any more than Blacks did back in the days when that was the law of the land. . . . Avoid "special" items like automatic door openers designed "for the handicapped," and instead buy the industry standard items that can work for everyone. You can save money, too, by avoiding things like "special" lavatory sinks. Do purchase sinks that

people in wheelchairs can get up to and use easily; do purchase lever-type faucets. But you don't have to pay more from medical suppliers for "special" plumbing. Any plumbing supply place can show you a range of items that work.

2. Create easy, independent access. In an effort to provide businesses with a great amount of flexibility, Congress didn't require (under ADA) measures that were costly or unduly burdensome. Congress allows, for example, for a waiter to read a menu to a diner with a visual impairment rather than providing a large-print or braille menu. While few people would object to being read a menu, a little thinking about this procedure makes you realize that it's less independent a method for a diner. It makes the diner "dependent" on someone else. This can't be helped in many cases. Nevertheless, when possible, your goal—much appreciated by disabled patrons—is to allow independent access. If you can afford the $5 or $6 to run to a quick-print place and have your menu enlarged by a photocopier to a large-print size, the solution offers more independence for those diners who can take advantage of this access option.

3. Make it work for everyone (or try to). Use common sense. Go beyond the minimum. Install a phone in a way that the greatest number of people can use it. Put in a door that the greatest number of people can get through independently. Add a door handle everybody can manipulate.

4. Apply the principle of "the most disabled user." When someone tells you what he or she needs for access, you might find it useful to ask: "Will this work best for people even more disabled than you? If I make it work for the most disabled user, will it work for you?"*

Finally, when thinking about universal design or any other design concept, "almost isn't good enough." A church with an accessible sanctuary is not an accessible church if there are no accessible restrooms. A church education building is not accessible if the only door to a room is twenty-nine inches wide and a person using a thirty-inch-wide wheelchair is trying to gain entry. A church conference on social justice and peacemaking is not very just if attendees can't navigate the way from the accessible hotel room to the accessible meeting site five long, bumpy, inaccessible sidewalk blocks away.

*Mary Johnson, *People with Disabilities Explain it All for You: Your Guide to the Public Accommodations Requirements of the American Disabilities Act* (Louisville: Avocado Press, 1992), pp. 51–56. Used with permission.

Accessibility Survey*

Use this list to review architectural barriers. Check for the following:

Parking and Paths

- Curb cuts to sidewalks and ramps to entrances
- Pathways at least 48 inches wide, with a slope of no more than 5 percent
- Level resting space around doors, 5 x 5 feet
- Marked accessible parking spaces close to accessible entrances

Ramps and Stairs

- Ramps 36 inches wide, minimum, extending 1 foot in length for every inch of rise, a 1:12 ratio. Thus, a ramp replacing an 8-inch step must extend 8 feet.
- Handrails on at least one side of the ramp, 32 inches above the surface.
- Protection over ramps from rain and snow, and nonskid surfaces
- Stairs with handrails on both sides, 32 inches above the step and extending a foot beyond the top and bottom of the stairs
- Stairs with rubber treads
- Slightly raised abrasive strips on top steps to warn people with limited sight where stairs begin

Doors and Doorways

- Door openings 32 inches wide or more
- Doors that can be opened by exerting 5 pounds of pressure
- Doors that can be opened electrically by the push of a button
- Lever handles or push bars

Worship Space

- Seating spaces with extra leg room for people using crutches, walkers, braces, or casts
- Scattered spaces or "pew cuts" for the users of wheelchairs who prefer to be seated in the main body of the congregation, not in the front or in the back of the sanctuary and not in the aisles. These pew cuts can easily be made by shortening several pews by 36 inches.
- Area with lectern and microphones accessible to those with mobility impairments

- Choir area allowing wheelchair users to participate
- Adequate lighting directed on the face of the speaker for those who read lips, as well as adequate general lighting in the sanctuary
- Book stands or lapboards available for those unable to hold prayer books, hymnals, or Bibles

Bathrooms

- At least one accessible bathroom, ideally one on each floor. These may be unisex, as in an airplane or a home.
- One toilet stall 36 inches wide, with 48 inches clear depth from door closing to front of commode and a 32-inch door that swings out
- Ideally, a 5 x 5 toilet stall with a 32-inch door that swings out and two grab bars, one adjacent to the commode and one behind the commode, to facilitate side transfer from a wheelchair
- A hospital or shower curtain providing privacy for wheelchair users, if metal dividers are removed and other renovations are not possible at the moment
- A sink with 29 inches of clearance from floor to bottom of the sink
- Towel dispensers no higher than 40 inches from the floor
- Lever-type faucet controls and hardware on doors

Water Fountains

- Water fountain mounted with basin no more than 36 inches from the floor, easily operated from wheelchairs
- As an interim measure, a supply of paper cups mounted next to the water fountain or a water cooler

Elevators and Lifts

- Elevators or chair lifts to ensure access to the sanctuary and all major program areas
- Controls placed at 54 inches or less from the elevator floor, reachable from a wheelchair
- Brailled plaques on elevator control panels
- A handrail on at least one side, 32 inches from the floor

*Ann Rose Davis and Ginny Thornburgh, *That All May Worship* (Washington, D.C.: National Organization on Disability, 1994), pp. 46–47. Used with permission.

How Can We Afford These Changes?*

Barbara Ramnaraine and Mary Jane Steinhagen, in their useful book *AccessAbility*, say: "Imagination, persistence, and social justice are the key elements in financing accessibility needs. For many in the congregation, building a ramp is not as exciting as installing a new organ. Remodeling to accommodate the needs of a few people does not capture the interest the same way erecting a new church can. Following are some thoughts for uniting your congregation behind an access project."

Principle #1:
Develop a Community Vision

The secret to successful financing seems to be in creating the largest vision possible of what is to be accomplished. This does not mean making the project expensive; it means making it comprehensive. Enlarging the parish's purpose to include community needs not only gives a project more stature; it may also make it eligible for outside funding from foundations interested in community service. Likewise, remodeling solely to satisfy requirements of people with disabilities does not encourage a congregation's support nearly as much as remodeling to improve the life of the whole parish by solving old space problems, creating new fellowship space, or making long-awaited repairs and improvements.

Principle #2:
Phase the Project

Develop a master plan that includes all the physical, program, and staff changes that may

---

IT SHALL BE SAID,
"BUILD UP, BUILD UP,
    PREPARE THE WAY,
    REMOVE EVERY
       OBSTRUCTION FROM MY
    PEOPLE'S WAY."
FOR THUS SAYS THE HIGH
    AND LOFTY ONE
    WHO INHABITS ETERNITY,
       WHOSE NAME IS HOLY:
I DWELL IN THE HIGH AND
    HOLY PLACE,
    AND ALSO WITH THOSE
       WHO ARE CONTRITE AND
    HUMBLE IN SPIRIT,
TO REVIVE THE SPIRIT OF THE
    HUMBLE,
    AND TO REVIVE THE HEART
    OF THE CONTRITE.

—ISA. 57:14–15

---

be contemplated in your congregation's future. Plan for the greatest likely extent of change and improvement. Include needs of people with disabilities, energy-saving ideas, more efficient space utilization, and expansion needs. Then break the plan into manageable stages, leading off, of course, with the essential access elements of the plan: ramps, bathroom, and accessible worship space.

Create independent stages of the project that might attract outside financing, such as an accessible meeting room for neighborhood needs, or an accessible office from which you may operate an outreach ministry to persons with disabilities in the neighborhood. There is always the chance that a particular part of the project will have special appeal to a progressive supporter: an elevator, a TTY machine, a new sound system.

Principle #3:
Explore All Funding Sources

If your project for ministry with people with disabilities has an important element of outreach into the community, you may be able to attract outside funding.

Some private foundations do grant funds for accessibility projects. Check your local library for additional foundation funding resources.

Accessibility projects intended primarily for the benefit of the congregation and its members will probably have to rely on internal funding sources and loans. Ways to raise funds within your own parish might include:

1. *Fund-Raisers*—Modest projects like temporary ramps, minor plumbing changes, and the like might be successfully funded from the usual array of bazaars, bake sales, dinners, and rummage sales. Every congregation has its secrets for success in this area.

2. *Endowment*—Congregations fortunate enough to have endowment and significant savings might consider using some of those resources

---

*Barbara Ramnaraine and Mary Jane Steinhagen, *AccessAbility: A Manual for Churches* (St. Paul, MN: Diocesan Office on Ministry with Persons Who Are Disabled of the Episcopal Diocese of Minnesota and Office for People with Disabilities, Catholic Charities of the Archdiocese of St. Paul, Minnesota, 1997), pp. 29–31. Used with permission.

to support accessibility needs. If principal funds are not available, consideration might be given to designating endowment interest for several years to supplement funding.

3. *Designated and Special Gifts*—Are there members of the congregation who might be willing to designate a portion of their estate for accessibility needs? Are some members of the congregation able to make significant contributions to a special project now?

4. *Capital Fund Drive*—A congregation might run a capital fund drive to raise money for accessibility needs.

Principle #4:
[Grantmanship] Is a Learnable Skill

The imaginative and persistent search for funds to make a facility accessible is a valid expression of good stewardship. Work hard at it. Seek professional help, or at least the assistance of folks within your congregation who have done fund-raising. Read and research methods of securing grants. Talk to other congregations about their funding successes and failures.

LYDIA GANS

Principle #5:
Don't Get Discouraged

It is estimated (on average) that you must submit ten grant applications before seeing results. All fund-raising is time consuming and slow-moving. Nevertheless, when your project is well developed and broadly based, it will inevitably succeed when you are persistent, when you believe in the validity of your mission, and when you keep your congregation interested and involved.

Funding Resources

Directory of Grants for Organizations Serving People with Disabilities. Richard M. Eckstein, ed. 1995. Research Grant Guides, P.O. Box 1214, Loxahatchee, FL 33470.

Fund Raiser's Guide to Human Service Funding. S. David Hicks, ed. 1993. The Taft Group, 12300 Twinbrook Parkway, Ste. 520, Rockville, MD 20852.

Fund Raiser's Guide to Religious Philanthropy. Bernard Jankowski, ed. 1994. The Taft Group, 12300 Twinbrook Parkway, Ste. 520, Rockville, MD 20852.

What Can My Church Do to Facilitate Removing Architectural Barriers?*

When beginning to make the architectural and structural changes necessary to welcome people with disabilities, start with things that can be accomplished relatively easily. Get under way! What you need are visible signs of change, not just lengthy committee meetings and handwringing.

It is true that aesthetic and historic preservation considerations must be taken into account as welcoming congregations make plans to adapt their buildings. And some of these adaptations will be expensive. It is not an acceptable argument, however, to delay because of "how few of 'them' we have." In God's realm, the number of users is not relevant!

Plan a fund-raising strategy that involves everyone, young and old, rich and not so rich. Think about everything from bake sales and

benefit dramas to (contributions for) expensive physical changes made in loving memory of a deceased relative. In addition, remember that some religious groups grant low-interest loans for these undertakings.

Begin by consulting members of the congregation and their relatives who are architects, contractors, carpenters, and plumbers. Their skills are needed and this is their day to shine! Don't forget to consult, in every phase of evaluation and planning, persons who are users of wheelchairs, walkers, crutches, and canes. By not doing so, many churches and synagogues have made well-intended but inadequate, even wasteful, changes. It goes without saying that all new construction or remodeling should meet current local access codes.

*Ann Rose Davis and Ginny Thornburgh, *That All May Worship* (Washington, D.C.: National Organization on Disability, 1994), p. 46. Used with permission.

Additional Resources

ADA Accessibility Guidelines regarding technical requirements/new construction are available from: Architectural and Transportation Barriers Compliance Board: 1-800-872-2253.

ADA Regional Disability and Business Technical Assistance Centers—call for a listing near you: 1-800-949-4232 (voice and TDD).

Adaptive Environments, Inc.
374 Congress Street, Ste. 301
Boston, MA 02210
Phone: (617) 695-1225 (voice and TDD)
Schools Hotline: 1-800-893-1225 (voice and TDD)
E-mail: www.adaptenv.org
Adaptive Environments promotes accessibility as well as universal design through education programs, technical assistance publications and design advocacy. Its mission is to eliminate barriers in housing, education, employment, recreational, and cultural life and to create environments that are accessible to all people.

Eastern Paralyzed Veterans Association
75-20 Astoria Blvd.
Jackson Heights, NY 11370
Toll-free: 1-800-444-0120
The Association provides ADA information and accessible building design information. Call or write to request their free publications list.

The Center for Universal Design
North Carolina State University
School of Design
P.O. Box 8613
Raleigh, NC 27695-8613
Phone: (919) 515-3082 (voice and TDD)
Toll-free: 1-800-647-6777, info requests
Fax: (919) 515-3023
E-mail: cud@ncsu.edu, URL: www2.ncsu.edu
The Center for Universal Design is a national research, information, and technical assistance center that evaluates, develops, and promotes accessible and universal design in buildings and related products.

Concrete Change
1371 Metropolitan Ave., SE
Atlanta, GA 30316
E-mail: Concrete Change@mindspring.com
Concrete Change is an organization that has long been active in promoting universal design and "visit-ability" in all homes. Much of their information is very useful to churches interested in barrier removal. They have a 15-minute video called *Building Better Neighborhoods* for $24.95 (postpaid). The video explains the importance of basic access to all homes. Visit their Web site at http://concretechange.home.mindspring.com for more information, or write them at the address above for information or to order the video.

6

In Service to the Church—Embracing Our Workers

" "

My congregation has embraced who I am as a little person.

> —Rev. Stella Dempski, associate pastor at
> First Presbyterian Church,
> Westminster, Maryland

" "

Persons who have disabilities can and do serve the church in a variety of ways, ranging from usher and committee member to pastor and seminary professor. A person with a disability is

NANCY ANNE DAWE

not asking for special favors. Keep in mind that she or he has managed to get around in the world and managed to negotiate the physical and attitudinal barriers during the course of getting an education. The individual has usually developed a fine set of problem-solving skills that enable as full an involvement with the world as possible—given the particulars of the person's disability.

The Rev. Stella Dempski was born with achondroplasia, a genetic disorder that results in several disabling conditions, including short stature. Before entering seminary, she worked

as a social worker after completing her undergraduate work. She thought because she had already spent time working in a professional capacity in the secular world, she would have no problem working for the church. She was surprised, therefore, at her initial difficulty in finding even an unpaid, ten-week internship. Throughout her life, she had successfully dealt with the stigmatism and stares because of her short stature and the rejection and subtle acts of discrimination. "What I expected from the church was grace and another type of attitude, and I didn't get that there. In fact, I got more grace from the secular world than the church itself. This (attitude) really didn't manifest itself until I got into seminary and was trying to seek out a call and flesh out my own ministry."

The church she now serves, however, chose to focus on her abilities and past work experience when hiring her for her current position, rather than making her disability an issue. A number of simple, low-cost accommodations have been implemented to help Rev. Dempski carry out her duties as associate pastor of education and discipleship. Stools are placed near the pulpit and throughout the church. Committee members understand that she is unable to sit for long periods of time during meetings and are accustomed to her standing up to stretch when necessary. Before she came to serve the church, the pastors passed Communion on large, heavy trays. She recognized that she would be unable to assist with this method, so another method of serving Communion was devised. Elders now come to her to receive the sacraments from the Communion table. These changes have both facilitated her ministry and made her feel very welcome.[1]

Fulfilling the Spirit of the Law

Employing Persons with Disabilities

Title I of the ADA, which covers employment, says, "Those involved in the religious ministry, such as ministers, priests, or rabbis, are not covered by Title I." Although this would seem to be fairly straightforward in its meaning, there is more that religious communities must be aware of when it comes to employing persons with disabilities, whether they are to serve as ministers or in some other capacity. Title I says that religious organizations, along with all businesses with fifteen or more employees are responsible for compliance with Title I requirements. (See appendixes 1 for Title I of the ADA.) The author of *Loving Justice*, a handbook about the religious community and ADA, says that "case law and the interpretation of the regulations are in flux. The statutory language of the ADA and its implementing regulations must be applied on a case-by-case basis."* The argument by many disability rights activists, however, is that the church is called by the higher mandate of God when it comes to employing persons with disabilities in *any* position in the church and that we, as the church, should be the model for the secular world.

The author of *Loving Justice* offers these additional tips regarding Title I of the ADA:

• Religious organizations with fifteen or more employees are responsible for compliance with Title I. . . . In most cases, religious employers can comply with ADA employment provisions through job restructuring, low-cost or no-cost accommodations, and rewriting job descriptions to highlight the essential functions of the position. As a first step, application forms should be reviewed and questions relating to disability be removed.

• Second, job descriptions should be developed that are based on the essential functions required to perform adequately in a given job. Such functional descriptions encourage a reliable comparison between the needs of the organization and the qualifications of an applicant, allowing both employer and applicant to have the exact requirements needed to fill a given position.

• The ADA prohibits preemployment inquiries about a disability, requiring that such inquiries be made in the post-offer stage of the hiring process. Before making a job offer, an employer: *may* ask questions about an applicant's ability to perform specific job functions; *may not* ask about a disability; *may* make a job offer that is conditioned on satisfactory results

of a post-offer medical examination or inquiry. During the initial interview process, leading questions seeking information about a possible disabling condition should be avoided. The following questions during this preemployment phase of the hiring process are inappropriate and illegal:

Do you have a disability?

Have you been treated for any of the following conditions or diseases?

How many days were you absent from work because of illness last year? (An employer may provide information on attendance requirements and ask if an applicant will be able to meet these requirements.)

Have you ever been treated for any mental condition?

• Interviewers may ask any number of questions related to the essential functions of the job and the applicant's ability to perform such tasks, as demonstrated by the following examples: "This job as office assistant will require you to file documents for approximately 10 percent of your time. The files are in cabinets at heights that range from floor level to five feet above the floor. Will you be able to do that?" A follow-up question might be: "What experience have you had in performing such a task?" Or: "This position of director of the Office on Disability Access will require you to spend approximately 25 percent of your time traveling around the area, visiting clergy and congregations, to educate and to monitor programs which ensure access. Are you able to travel and keep these appointments?" A follow-up question might be: "You say you need a driver to keep your appointments in areas not served by public transportation. How has this worked for you in the past?"

• After making a conditional job offer and before an individual starts work, an employer may conduct a medical examination to ask health-related questions, providing that all candidates who receive a conditional job offer in the same job category are required to take the same examination and/or respond to the same inquiries. *Note:* If the medical examination or inquiry screens out an individual with a disability, the employer will need to show that the exam is job-related and consistent with business necessity and that the job performance cannot be accomplished with a reasonable accommodation.

*Ginny Thornburgh, *Loving Justice: The ADA and the Religious Community* (Washington, D.C.: National Organization on Disability, 1994), pp. 9–10. Used with permission.

Hiring and Including Persons with Disabilities in Church Leadership

As a Presbyterian Church we are not necessarily exempt under Title I of the ADA when it comes to employment of persons with disabilities. The *Book of Order* was amended in 1993 to forbid discrimination against persons with disabilities in calling persons to ministerial leadership (G-11.0502g). The National Capital Presbytery Policy extends this to "provide equal opportunity and *mobility* in employment for all qualified persons in all job categories with the presbytery" (italics added). In addition, the presbytery "will prohibit discrimination in employment because of race, color, national origin, sex, age, marital status, or *disability* by searching out and eliminating all causes leading to adverse impact." National Capital Presbytery has devised a supplement to its EEOC hiring policies, a portion of which follows (see page 53 for more information):

> Reasonable accommodation is any change or adjustment to a job or work environment that permits a qualified applicant or employee with a disability to participate in the job application process, to perform the essential functions of a job, or to enjoy benefits and privileges of employment equal to those enjoyed by employees without disabilities. For example, reasonable accommodation may include:
>
> • acquiring or modifying equipment or devices
>
> • job restructuring
>
> • part-time or modified work schedules
>
> • reassignment to a vacant position
>
> • adjusting or modifying examinations, training materials or policies
>
> • providing readers and interpreters
>
> • making the workplace readily accessible to and usable by people with disabilities

The Presbytery of the Twin Cities Area has had an active Disabilities Concerns Committee for a number of years. They adopted a policy statement in 1998 regarding the full participation of persons with disabilities in the activities of the presbytery. The policy statement (contact the presbytery office at the address listed at the end of this chapter for the complete policy) of the Presbytery of the Twin Cities Area makes the following provisions:

1. Affirms the commitment of the Presbyterian Church (U.S.A.) to full participation of persons with disabilities.

2. Provides support to its member congregations as they modify facilities, programs, and policies to include persons with disabilities.

3. Bears witness to its support of a policy of inclusiveness by:
   a. Holding meetings of the presbytery and its councils and committees in accessible facilities.
   b. Providing, when requested, materials in alternative formats.
   c. Providing, when requested, in a timely manner, signers for meetings and events sponsored by the Presbytery of the Twin Cities Area.
   d. Strongly recommending that all loan requests for funding new construction or remodeling of church property include provisions for accessibility.
   e. Strongly recommending that all programs funded by grants from the presbytery include specific provisions regarding accessibility.

The Presbytery of Long Island adopted a similar policy statement, "So That All May Participate." This policy statement has served as a model for other presbyteries, most recently the Presbytery of Hudson River. Your presbytery can devise its own policy statement or use the resources here as models.

Seminary and Ordination Exams

Within the Office of the General Assembly is the Department of Constitutional Services which administers ordination exams to those who want to be ordained to ministry of the Word and Sacrament. The Rev. Jerry Houchens is the Associate for Presbyteries' Cooperative Committees on Examination and says provisions regarding disabilities are included. "Anyone with a disability shall be accommodated in order to make the examination experience meaningful for them." In order to achieve this goal, a three-way approach is required with the presbytery, Jerry's office, and the candidate all working together to make the examination have integrity for the candidate and the church as well. Mr. Houchens says, "Persons with disabilities need to be approved by their presbytery (and a decision reached) as to how the presbytery wishes to accommodate the candidate." Depending on the nature of the person's disability, the exam may be an oral exam, or the examination time may be extended, but the accommodations are always highly individual.

Princeton Theological Seminary used this three-way approach to develop a precedent-setting policy regarding disability and ordination. The Committee on Preparation for Ministry was faced with a unique challenge. One of Princeton's students is dyslexic, and unable to fulfill the language requirements for ordination because of his disability. In 1997, a subcommittee was established to research dyslexia and to put together a recommendation and policy statement dealing with persons with disabilities and the completion of the language requirements for ordination. The policy was submitted to the candidate's presbytery for consideration in June of 1998 (see appendix 3) and was approved without amendment, and with a standing ovation by the Presbytery of New Brunswick.

Planning Accessible Meetings

In addition to its paid workers, the Presbyterian Church (U.S.A.) has a rich legacy that includes laity in decision making and in carrying out God's work on behalf of the church. Given the fact that there are an estimated 43 million persons with disabilities in the United States, we can assume that a percentage of these persons are Presbyterians who participate at every level in the life of the church. Consider the population of persons with disabilities as a great, largely untapped resource of talents and gifts. With a little effort and planning, churches, presbyteries, and synods can include persons with disabilities in leadership roles in our churches. Long Island Presbytery had for several years in its budget a line item for inclusion and participation of persons on its committees. Persons with disabilities could be reimbursed for baby-sitting services, cost of taxi or other accessible transportation, cost for interpreters or signers, cost of brailling and audiotaping—all paid for from this budget. Presbyterians for Disabilities Concerns has allowed in its budget

monies to pay for many of the items mentioned previously, and for attendant services for team members who attend overnight meetings.

For leaders planning meetings, it is safe to assume that someone with a disability will attend the meeting. Advance publicity should clearly indicate that your meeting will be accessible. When sending out registration information, provide space on the form for persons with disabilities to specify what accommodations will be needed. Accommodations may include special diet, materials made available in alternative media, or wheelchair-accessible or scent-free meeting and hotel rooms, and may even include making decisions about attendant or personal-care assistants, to name a few. (See appendix 4 for a sample registration form.)

After the registration form is received, someone from the planning team will want to contact persons who are requesting accommodations to ensure that needs will be met and that communication lines are open. The person requesting materials in braille, for example, may be able to tell you best where to find a provider. A person who is deaf may be able to tell planners where to find a sign language interpreter.

If the meeting involves an overnight stay, plan on using the Universal Design concept outlined in chapter 5 (page 40)—choose the most accessible hotel that will meet the needs of the most people who are attending your meeting. Many hotels these days are in compliance with ADA requirements. However, when hotel reservationists assure you their rooms are accessible, don't necessarily take their word for it. A wheelchair user attending a meeting at a local hotel in Louisville was assured by hotel management that the rooms were accessible. When the attendee arrived, she found that she could not get her wheelchair through the bathroom door. Management had to have the door and door frame removed—which doesn't really allow for much privacy when sharing a room. Better for planners to check out both the hotel and meeting site well in advance of sending out any meeting materials. Planners will want to make sure, also, that someone at the hotel will see to access needs, particularly if they have been promised. Following are a few additional factors to consider when choosing hotels:

- The ADA Accessibility Guidelines state that the "minimum" space requirements for a bathroom are 36 x 48 inches. Be advised that these are minimum requirements and that wheelchairs do come in larger sizes. At 36 x 48 inches, there is barely enough space to maneuver with even the smallest wheelchair. When possible, try to choose hotels and meeting sites that have bathrooms larger than required and plenty of maneuvering space in other rooms as well.

- An accessible bathroom needs grab bars and a toilet seat that is of the correct height. The ADA Accessibility Guidelines recommend that grab bars be installed 36 inches up from the floor. Maneuvering is easier if there are grab bars on either side of the toilet. A great variance in the toilet-height needs of people with disabilities exists. If the toilet seat is not high enough for someone, management should be able to easily find a seat riser from a local medical supply center or center for accessible living.

- An accessible hotel bathroom should have a tub or shower area that can be accessed by a person in a wheelchair, as well as by others with disabilities. When choosing hotels, look for bathrooms with "drive-in" showers stalls with plenty of room and that have a seat and grab bars in them.

- An accessible hotel bathroom has both its toilet paper dispenser and soap dispenser within easy reach. In addition, the vanity should provide pull-up space for people who use wheelchairs. Lever faucets on sinks and showers or bathtubs are better than round knobs because they are easier to turn on and off.

- Light switches should be located at a height that can be accessed easily by people who use wheelchairs. As mentioned earlier, rocker switches are easier to manipulate than the conventional switches.

- A telephone is accessible (for example, near the bed, so a person can get to it easily while in bed) to a person who uses a wheelchair, but may not be accessible to a person who is hard of hearing or deaf. Choose hotels that have TDDs available for those who need them.

- Choose hotels that have raised numbers on the door and that use conventional keys or magnetic cards with raised marks on them indicating correct point of insertion into computerized locks. Accessible hotels will also have braille signage on elevators and exits and on all material that is available to sighted people, such as a menu.

- Choose hotels that have plenty of nearby grassy areas in which to walk guide dogs.

The preceding information should also apply when choosing a meeting site. Planners may also want to have a designated "access station" on the day of registration and following, complete with a staff person or volunteer to work out any glitches that may arise. Whenever possible, the meeting site should be in the same building as the hotel. For larger gatherings, this may simply not be possible. Try to choose a meeting site as close as possible and make sure the route between hotel and meeting site is a clear route (no cracks in sidewalks or construction zones that can be hazardous to persons with a variety of disabilities). Sidewalks should have curb cuts so wheelchair users can maneuver from the sidewalk in order to cross streets. If it is absolutely necessary to choose a meeting site that is a great distance from the hotel, planners will want to make sure that paratransit or accessible transportation is available, not just between hotel and meeting site, but also from airport to hotel— and well in advance of the event.

A note about paratransit and accessible public transportation: Requirements for use of paratransportation varies from state to state and even city to city. Planners will want to contact the public transportation provider in the city where the meeting is to be held and ask them for details. Some cities require that the person requiring paratransit service provide verification from their home state that they are "Paratransit certified." Most providers require advance reservation of paratransit vehicles and the advance reservation can be as much as two weeks or as little as a few hours. Paratransit can sometimes be spontaneously arranged on weekends when there is less use from the local population. Be advised, also, that accessible public transportation usually has a very specific and often limited route, which may have restrictions for users or may not have service available during the times a meeting is arranged. Planners will want to get specific information about this from the transportation provider in the city where the meeting is to be held, well in advance of the event.

✔✔✔

What Can My Synod, Presbytery, and Church Do to Serve Our Workers Who Become Disabled?*

Another area that we need to consider is that of our workers who become disabled during their term of service to the church. When a pastor or other paid church worker becomes seriously ill or disabled, presbyteries and their executive staff need to return to the "model" of being "pastor to pastors." The early model of executive was to have a person who was pastoral—a true bishop, function as a pastor to pastors. Fifty percent of their time was to be spent on this pastoral function—the other 50 percent was to be spent promoting the benevolence program of the denomination. This model worked for both the pastors under their care and for the benevolence program.

A pastor-to-pastor model carries some requirements:

- *Knowledge of and care for the ministers and their families within the presbytery*—This means getting out of the office and into the homes and churches, developing a caring relationship that makes the executive a true friend and not an adversary or one to be feared for the power he/she possesses.

- *A system of care that includes being in on the ground floor of need*—Calls in the hospitals are absolutely essential. The pastoral presence of someone officially representing the presbytery is only a first step. There must be follow-up with home calls and a genuine concern for the needs of the entire family. In this early process, telephone calls will not suffice. There must also be personal visits.

- *Correct information about pension benefits, Social Security benefits*—and how the two interact, plus knowledge of other agencies and services that might be of assistance.

- *Sensitivity to the pastor's financial situation*—Those offering assistance must know how to

> WHAT DOES THE LORD REQUIRE OF YOU BUT TO DO JUSTICE, AND TO LOVE KINDNESS, AND TO WALK HUMBLY WITH YOUR GOD?
>
> —MIC. 6:8

serve that need, and all must be accomplished in a timely manner. Every effort must be made to assure the pastor and his or her family that they will not be removed from that pastorate (or home) until such time as all involved know that there is no other alternative.

- *Flexibility in dealing with extended or medical leave*—If churches find this to be a financial burden, the presbytery could offer to pay for the pulpit supply until such time as a final resolution is made. Presbyteries should also be able to see to it that the churches allow enough time for a family to make a transition without feeling as if they are being forced out.

- *Education about disability*—A physical disability does not mean that the call to serve has also been removed! Nor has the desire to preach—nor the call of God. A minister who becomes disabled can still serve his or her church.

- *Efforts to supplement salaries for ministers with disabilities who are able to return to work part-time or return to limited schedules*—At the present time, there is no middle ground. Both Social Security and the Board of Pension's programs allow only for the disabled or the nondisabled. That could be changed to the advantage of both the minister and the church. The Board of Pensions might even find it financially advantageous.

Finally, the bottom line is simply the willingness to break the status quo. Of all institutions in the world, the church of Jesus Christ should be the most loving and compassionate—the most willing to live out what it means to be Christlike in all its dealings, particularly its dealings with its own shepherds.

*Dr. David Castrodale. Used with permission.

Additional Resources

A Guide to Planning Accessible Meetings, by June Isaacson Kailes and Darrell Jones, is written for businesses who hold meetings and want to comply with ADA guidelines. Very applicable to church meetings, with sections on site selection, communications access, registration forms, and more. It is available in regular print and on audiotape for $25. (Can order from ILRU. See below.)

Job Accommodation Network (JAN) —an information network for employers to discuss solutions for accommodating workers. Toll-free: 1-800-526-7234.

Loving Justice: The ADA and the Religious Community costs $10 per single copy (price break for multiple copies) and can be ordered from: Religion and Disability Program, National Organization on Disability (N.O.D.), 910 16th Street, NW, Washington, DC 20006; phone: (202) 293-5960; voice: (202) 293-5968; (TDD); e-mail: www.nod.org.

Independent Living Research Utilization (ILRU) Program
2323 South Shepherd, Suite 1000,
Houston, TX 77019
Phone: (713) 520-0232 (voice)
(713) 520-5136 (TDD)
Fax: (713) 520-5785
URL: www.ilru.org
The ILRU is a national center for information, training, research, and technical assistance in independent living and has been around since 1977! A majority of the staff are people with disabilities who serve independent living centers, state and federal rehabilitation agencies, consumer organizations, and related organizations. It is an excellent resource for just about any information about disability. They produce a number of fine publications such as a comprehensive directory of over 400 programs providing independent living services in the U.S. ($10.00) and a brochure that gives an overview of the independent living movement and its philosophy, and explains what services independent living centers offer and where to find the centers ($.50). They sponsor an extensive, user-friendly "on-line library of independent

living-related resource materials that have been developed by staff at independent living centers and other organizations involved in the independent living and disability rights movements over the years." If you are new to disability, start here for your search for on-line information at www.dimenet.com/ilrulib.

"So That All May Participate," the policy statement for including persons with disabilities, can be requested from: Stated Clerk, Presbytery of Long Island, 42 Hauppauge Rd., Commack, NY 11725; phone: (516) 499-7171; fax: (516) 499-7063.

Complete policy statement on disabilities by the Presbytery of the Twin Cities Area can be requested from: Stated Clerk, The Presbytery of the Twin Cities Area, 122 W. Franklin Ave., Rm 508, Minneapolis, MN 55404-2467; phone: (612) 871-7281 (voice); fax: (612) 871-0698; PresbyNet Inbox: PBY TWIN CITIES AREA.

Supplement to the National Capital Presbytery Policy on EEO/AA for Persons with Disabilities can be requested from: Stated Clerk, National Capital Presbytery, 4915 45th Street NW, Washington, DC 20016-2790; phone: (202) 244-4760 (voice); fax: (202) 244-9688; PresbyNet Inbox: PBY NATIONAL CAPITAL.

Questions regarding disability and the ordination exam can be sent to Jerry Houchens, Associate for Presbyteries' Cooperative Committees on Examination, Office of the General Assembly, PCUSA, Department of Constitutional Services, Rm 4430, 100 Witherspoon St., Louisville, KY 40202; phone: (502) 569-5748.

To learn more about the process of developing a policy like "Biblical Languages: Learning Disabilities and an Alternative Course of Study," contact: David Wall, Program Coordinator, Center of Continuing Education, Princeton Theological Seminary, 20 Library Place, Princeton, NJ 08540; phone: (609) 497-7990 or 1-800-622-6767, ext. 7990; e-mail: david.wall@ptsem.edu.

Additional Resources

Organizations and Publications Concerned with Disability Rights

ADAPT
P.O. Box 9595
Denver, CO 80209
Phone: (303) 333-6698
E-mail: www.adapt.org
ADAPT (American Disabled for Attendant Services Today) "has a history of organizing in the disability community and using civil disobedience and similar nonviolent direct action tactics to achieve its goals." ADAPT, formerly called American Disabled for Accessible Public Transit, was organized in the early 1980s to address the issue of the lack of accessible public transportation. ADAPT was instrumental in gaining passage of the Americans with Disabilities Act. Currently, the organization focuses on "promoting services in the community instead of warehousing people with disabilities in institutions and nursing homes. Attendant services (help with things like eating, dressing, toileting, moving from wheelchair to bed, etc.) are the cornerstone to community-based services for people with severe disabilities. ADAPT is working to get 25 percent of the Medicaid long-term care funds redirected to pay for a national, mandated attendant services program."

CIL Berkeley
2539 Telegraph Ave.
Berkeley, CA 94704
Phone: (510) 841-4776
(510) 841-3101 (TDD)
Fax: (510) 841-6168
E-mail: http://www.cilberkeley.org

CIL Oakland
436 14th St., Ste. 218
Oakland, CA 94612
Phone: (510) 763-9999, (510) 444-1837 (TDD)
Fax: (510) 763-4910
The Center for Independent Living (CIL) is a national leader in helping people with disabilities live independently and become productive, fully participating members of society. The staff and board, most of whom have disabilities, are strongly committed to supporting others in their efforts toward self-sufficiency. Since 1972 we have opened doors for over 140,000 people, who were traditionally viewed only as "patients," to help them leave institutions, set up independent living situations, and hold jobs.

DREDF
2212 Sixth St.
Berkeley, CA 94710
Phone: (510) 644-2555 (Voice/TDD)
Fax: (510) 841-8645
E-Mail: dredf@dredf.orgwww.dredf.org
DREDF (The Disability Rights Education and Defense Fund) was founded in 1979 by people with disabilities and parents of children with disabilities. It is a national law and policy center dedicated to protecting and advancing the civil rights of people with disabilities through legislation, litigation, advocacy, technical assistance, and education and training of attorneys, and advocates.

No Pity: People with Disabilities Forging a New Civil Rights Movement, by Joseph P. Shapiro. New York: Random House, Inc., 1994. Paperback, $15.00. A very readable and interesting account of the fight for equal rights by and for persons with disabilities by a social policies writer for *U.S. News & World Report*.

The Ragged Edge, ed. Barrett Shaw. Louisville: Advocado Press, Inc., 1994. Paperback, $18.95. Order from your local bookstore or directly from the publisher: P.O. Box 145, Louisville, KY 40201. The book was named an "outstanding book on the subject of human rights in North America" by the Gustavus Myers Center for the Study of Human Rights. This book tells readers what it is like to be a person with a disability in America today. The Advocado Press also publishes a bimonthly magazine, *Ragged Edge*, which keeps it's finger on the pulse of the disability experience in America. $17.50/year for individuals; organizational fee is $35.00. Send your order to the address above or visit their Web site at www.ragged-edge-mag.com.

7

A Discussion about Disability

“ ”

I am . . . Presbyterian and have a 1996 M.Div. from San Francisco Presbyterian Seminary. I use a manual wheelchair because of the bone disorder osteogenesis imperfecta (colloquially known as "the brittle bone disease"). There are major theological issues and political issues that are important in (including persons with disabilities in the life of the church). These issues are both complicated and difficult—for all concerned. To pique your interest, let me say that many people, both within and outside the church, want disabled people to be "nicer than Jesus."

—Lynn Park, member of
St. John's Presbyterian Church,
Berkeley, California

“ ”

In God's Image*

Of the many questions pastors receive in ministry, the hardest to answer is always "Why? Why, Lord, Why?" How any of us answers this question shapes the whole of our lives, our faith, and our relationship to God. This question is usually raised with tears in the eyes that reflect the hurt and the sorrow in the heart. It is raised when someone young dies, perhaps a child or a teenager. It comes when cancer or another terminal illness is diagnosed. It comes when a job is lost. The question comes in the reality of disability. The question rises every time we are hurting.

As a chaplain at Polk Center, a large facility for persons with mental retardation, I met a young woman who set my mind spinning on the theology of disabilities. While I was spending some time with her in her cottage, she looked at me, and with all sincerity in her eyes, asked: "What did I do that is so *bad* that God did this to me?" This is a hard question. The first thing that all of us must come to terms with is that even if we are Christians—even Presbyterians—our faith does not make us immune to tragedy. Instead, our faith prepares us to face each difficult event in our lives with the assurance of a God who loves us, a God who enables and strengthens us in all things.

People bring their own faith perspectives to the difficult times in their lives. Theological studies reveal that there are at least seven different ways people of faith answer the difficult question of why. The seven answers are the following:

1. It is God's will.
2. It is punishment for sin.
3. It is a test of faith.
4. It is an opportunity for character development.
5. It is a manifestation of the power of God.
6. It is redemptive suffering.
7. It is God's mysterious omnipotence.

For the young woman with mental retardation to ask what she had done that was so wrong for God to cause her difficulties, raises

*The Reverend Sue Montgomery is a graduate of Maryville College, Maryville, Tennessee, with a degree in philosophy and religion and a music minor. She graduated from Pittsburgh Theological Seminary with an M. Div. in 1977. In 1997, she received the Women's Ministries General Assembly "Accompanying the Voiceless" Woman of Faith Award for her advocacy work in many areas, particularly in the area of disability concerns. Recently she led a series of workshops for chaplains in the Commonwealth of Pennsylvania on the theology of disabilities and is leading a retreat for Presbyterian Women on the theologies of disability and limitations.

the pain, the cruelty of always equating sin with disability. We can see the consequences of wrongdoing and pain when a parent bends a child's arm hard enough in anger and it breaks. The consequences are obvious. But for a person to be born with disabilities, birth defects, to say it is God's will, to say that child is God's special chosen one, creates even more pain for the family and for the child as she or he seeks to live a life in relationship to a God of love. God does not will suffering on those whom God loves and names as family.

Throughout history, disability and illness have been associated with sin. If you read the biography of Franklin Delano Roosevelt *FDR's Splendid Deception* (Arlington, VA: Vandamere Press, 1994), by Hugh Gregory Gallagher, you'll see how the understanding of sin and disability made FDR hide the polio that had paralyzed his lower body. Prejudice and misunderstandings continue to fuel the myths and fears that build unnecessary barriers between persons with disabilities and the ablebodied.

Our faith does *not* provide us with an insurance policy that protects or insures us against the possibility of facing tragic events. Persons within the disability community are well aware that even the ablebodied are only temporarily abled. An accident can create disability in a matter of seconds, and if illness or disease doesn't create a disability, old age will. A healthy theology of disability equips us to handle each difficult period or event in our lives with faith. A healthy theology does not paralyze us with false platitudes and demeaning words of wisdom that only make others feel better. Rather, a healthy theology lifts up the assurance, the promise, that no matter what happens in life we are *never* alone. Our theological understanding of disability gives shape and form to our faith and our lives. Our theology should not become an additional disability; rather our theology should set us free to be the people God created us to be.

There are never any easy or sure answers to the question "Why?" No one of the seven answers on page 55 is acceptable by itself. Most people apply a combination of them. One thing that will always remain true is that God is a God of love. God's love enables us to take whatever difficult times we have and live in hope and in God's grace. Our Christian faith is unique in that what lies at the heart of our theology is the belief that the crucifixion of Jesus became the greatest gift God could give. Through the crucifixion come the gifts of resurrection and eternal life. We must never forget: We cannot claim the resurrection until we claim the crucifixion. We cannot claim forgiveness until we claim the cross. It is by faith that we take the disability and turn it into a blessing. Without a faith decision, the disability cannot be named a blessing. Without a faith decision, disability cannot be used to glorify God.

Persons with disabilities and their families have to travel that journey of faith. It is the responsibility of the church to provide a healthy theology of disabilities. For too long the theology of disabilities has been defined by the ablebodied, and it has been oppressive to persons with disabilities. It is time to hear the voices of persons with disabilities. We have the capability of thinking theologically; our stories as well as our voices need to be heard in the theological process.

As persons with disabilities begin thinking theologically, we need to explore the question of what it means to be created in the image of God. If we are created in the image of God, then we have a God who understands disability, a God who knows, a God who walks—or rolls—with persons who are physically disabled, a God who speaks in sign language with persons who are hearing impaired, a God who sees with the fingertips and other senses as does a person who is blind, a God who tells us all we are the family of God, God's own. If we think about it, when God finished with the creation, God stood back, saw what was created, and pronounced it good—God didn't pronounce it perfect! To be created in the image of God is to be who we are, and in the presence of God we are accepted unconditionally. Although our bodies may be different and we may do things through adaptive equipment or with alternative skills, our gifts are many. Our gifts are desired by God, our lives are welcomed—and blessed in faith.

Study Questions

1. The future remains an unknown reality. An auto accident, a stroke can change our lives in seconds. How would your faith support you and in what ways would your faith shape your life in the face of disability? Imagine yourself no longer able to walk, see, or hear—what would you say to God in prayer?

2. Theology gives shape and form to our faith and the way we live out our lives. What is your theology regarding suffering? Would your theology change if you faced the loss of your independence and ability to function in normal ways?

Teaching a Church to "Be With"*

The Teamwork of God and John

This is the story of John, whom I met when he was about to be "deinstitutionalized" from a state institution for people with developmental disabilities. John was then in his mid-twenties and had been institutionalized for seven years after living in many foster homes and various group home arrangements. And he was placed into this specific institution because they had no other idea of where to put him.

John spent much of his life in a wheelchair, limited in his mobility due to cerebral palsy. He was also dyslexic, having a reading disability. Through acceptance of some of his limitations because of his disabilities, John wanted to explore the broader realm of his capacities outside the figurative and literal walls of the institution. While John cannot read or write without some difficulties, John can memorize, listen, and tell a good story.

One of the stories John tells well is of his varied experiences with churches. He has attended both mainline denominational and nondenominational churches, from traditional to preachers who are snake handlers. He remembers first taking God seriously when he was thirteen years old. And the reason he first believed God loved him was because he didn't die in all his moves to various homes, foster families, and finally to institutional care.

His worst memory was of a pastor of a small church who was sure that John's disability was caused by the devil. When they tried to exorcise the devil, John was sure they were going to exorcise him.

By contrast, when John discovered a small

*Brett Webb-Mitchell is assistant professor of Christian nurture at Duke University Divinity School and is an ordained pastor in the Presbyterian Church (U.S.A.). He is also the author of *God Plays Piano Too: The Spiritual Lives of Disabled Children* (New York: Crossroad, 1993); *Unexpected Guests at God's Banquet: Welcoming People with Disabilities into the Church* (New York: Crossroad, 1994); and *Dancing with Disabilities: Opening the Church to All God's Children* (Cleveland: United Church Press, 1997).

congregation of Christians who accepted him for who he was, a child of God, John began to learn some of the ways to live with himself in Christ's body, limitations and all. Exclaimed John: "They talk to me as if I really had a brain! Others who come here (to the institution), oh, they just talk to us adults as if we were really little kids; it drives me crazy."

In the institution, John lives with many others who experience open rejection by other people around them, contributing to a gross loss of self-image, because of their disabling conditions. It is within the context of the church that John has discovered not only how smart he can be, but also how foolish he can be on other days: "I'm so damn stupid, as we all are." For John, such insight or self-awareness comes from his continuous struggle in learning to live with his disabilities in a world and church that considers itself "nondisabled," which, as a result, actually taught him the virtue of courage of character:

> If you took away my disability, I probably couldn't tell stories. It's all teamwork between God and myself. I've looked back on this disability. I probably would've been wilder without the disability. But the disability gives me strength. I ask God to continue to give me the energy to get around. And I do that pretty well with the wheelchair. The disability used to get me down because I used to be so slow. But people who think I can't do anything from this (chair) are always surprised when God and I get together. It's OK for you to prevent my getting hurt, but don't prevent God and John from doing things together.[1]

What John discovered about himself, with his limitations amid a congregation of Christians who were at best discreet about their limitations and at worst in denial, was the Christian virtue of courage. This kind of courage is perhaps best described by Catholic theologian Herbert McCabe, O. P. :

> Courage is a disposition of our feelings of aggression which inclines us, characteristically, to face up to and deal with difficulties and dangers for the sake of doing what is good: a courageous person is neither overaggressive nor timid; is angry about the right things at the right time and is prepared to suffer patiently when it is necessary, and even to die for the sake of justice or in witness to the gospel.
>
> We exercise the virtue of courage principally in energetic struggle on behalf of the poor and

the weak and on every occasion when we have to face hostility and danger for the sake of justice and the gospel.[2]

What I discovered in being with John is a man who embodies the Christian virtue of courage. John is the very person some in the world would consider poor and weak, facing hostility and danger, even at the hands of some Christians. Yet, he teaches me, teaches us, courage. For John continues to enjoy life, even when, at times, his life has been anything but smooth sailing. He has lived through torturous conditions in some foster family arrangements; thrived in a state institution for people with developmental disabilities, even though he himself is not mentally retarded; and continues to believe in the goodness of God in Christ even in churches wanting to exorcise either him or

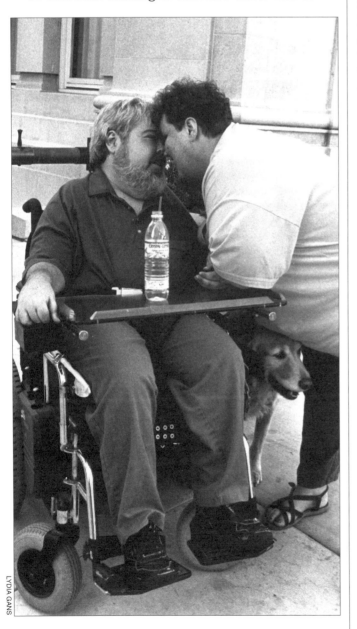

LYDIA GANS

the devil, or both. He suffered patiently as people learned to be with John in his limitations, his frustrations, his anger toward family and God, and the too-few times of joy with other congregations who didn't understand him. Finally, John triumphed over "do-gooders" in churches, who wanted to rescue John from his life, who felt sorry for John. John would admit that he is good at complaining. John now knows that when he hears the words "We're here to help you," it's a warning to run—or wheel oneself—in a different direction.

John finally discovered a congregation willing to learn a way of listening to John as John located what he himself needed and wanted. Finding a congregation that was willing to learn to be with John as *John* was learning to be with himself was a gift. John was given hope in the places in which he was challenged with life. This was a congregation that, rather than assuming they knew best what John desired, was formed well in the practice of hospitality. They were capable of discerning John's place in the ongoing life of the body of Christ by being *with* John first, and walking *with* John on the pilgrimage toward God's dominion rather than walking *for* John, or *on* John, for that matter. Such damage, such wrong, is hard to undo.

While John does not readily acknowledge or describe in great detail the congregation of which he is a member, they nevertheless matter in John's story. Again, this congregation was practicing the grace-initiated gesture of being *with* John in his hurt, his abuse, his limitations. One of the primary problems for many congregations in welcoming people with disabling conditions is learning to provide the place and time and good company to utter the words and practice the gestures of Christian courage. In other words, the problem is that most congregations are willing to care *for* and to do things for the person with a disabling condition, regardless of what the person with a disability may need, rather than first *being with* the one who simply needs the good company of the other sisters and brothers in Christ, who can lend support when needed or asked. The church has a tendency to act like a gathering that is more like Jesus' friend, Martha.

Let me explain: In the Gospel According to Luke at chapter 10:38–42, Jesus is visiting his friends, the sisters Mary and Martha. On the one hand, there is Mary, the one sitting at Jesus' feet, listening to what he is saying. She is the one practicing the art of being with Jesus, giving him her undivided attention. Martha, on the other hand, is "distracted by her many tasks." So exasperated is Martha by her decision to do all the work that she asks Jesus: "Lord, do you not care that my sister has left me to do all the work by myself? Tell her then to help me." But Jesus replies: "Martha, Martha, you are worried and distracted by many things; there is need of only one thing. Mary has chosen the better part, which will not be taken away from her."

We, the church, are like a gathering of Marthas when it comes to Jesus in the lives of people with disabling conditions. At first glance, it is Martha's arrogance of self-determination that keeps her from being fully with Jesus. Afraid to acknowledge our very being is sin, made insecure by the fragileness of human life, scarred by our mortal wounds, we wear masks that shout, "I'm OK, so you be OK, OK?" We take refuge and try to remain hidden by keeping busy, or distracted in tending to the needs we impose on the disability of the other person. Not wanting to feel as if we are dependent on anyone else in life, yet not wanting to feel out of control, we force our good works on those with the disabling conditions, whether "they" want "our" help or not, just like Martha.

Mary, so Jesus tells us, chose the better part. Unlike Martha, Mary sat at Jesus' feet and listened to what he was saying. Mary not only heard the words, but listened with her body and spirit to Jesus. Mary was dependent on Jesus. Mary was practicing the hospitality of *being with* Jesus. She must have been hanging on every word that Jesus said to her. Whereas Martha couldn't hear it, because she was so busy and not open to the word of God, Mary was open to receiving the good news, Jesus Christ.

The task before us Christians is to be more like Mary than Martha as we teach the church to *be with* the one with a disabling condition and his or her family and friends; it is to practice the gesture of *being with* Jesus. On the one hand, if

Bᴜᴛ ᴡᴇ ʜᴀᴠᴇ ᴛʜɪꜱ ᴛʀᴇᴀꜱᴜʀᴇ ɪɴ ᴄʟᴀʏ ᴊᴀʀꜱ, ꜱᴏ ᴛʜᴀᴛ ɪᴛ ᴍᴀʏ ʙᴇ ᴍᴀᴅᴇ ᴄʟᴇᴀʀ ᴛʜᴀᴛ ᴛʜɪꜱ ᴇxᴛʀᴀᴏʀᴅɪɴᴀʀʏ ᴘᴏᴡᴇʀ ʙᴇʟᴏɴɢꜱ ᴛᴏ Gᴏᴅ ᴀɴᴅ ᴅᴏᴇꜱ ɴᴏᴛ ᴄᴏᴍᴇ ꜰʀᴏᴍ ᴜꜱ. Wᴇ ᴀʀᴇ ᴀꜰꜰʟɪᴄᴛᴇᴅ ɪɴ ᴇᴠᴇʀʏ ᴡᴀʏ, ʙᴜᴛ ɴᴏᴛ ᴄʀᴜꜱʜᴇᴅ; ᴘᴇʀᴘʟᴇxᴇᴅ, ʙᴜᴛ ɴᴏᴛ ᴅʀɪᴠᴇɴ ᴛᴏ ᴅᴇꜱᴘᴀɪʀ; ᴘᴇʀꜱᴇᴄᴜᴛᴇᴅ, ʙᴜᴛ ɴᴏᴛ ꜰᴏʀꜱᴀᴋᴇɴ; ꜱᴛʀᴜᴄᴋ ᴅᴏᴡɴ, ʙᴜᴛ ɴᴏᴛ ᴅᴇꜱᴛʀᴏʏᴇᴅ; ᴀʟᴡᴀʏꜱ ᴄᴀʀʀʏɪɴɢ ɪɴ ᴛʜᴇ ʙᴏᴅʏ ᴛʜᴇ ᴅᴇᴀᴛʜ ᴏꜰ Jᴇꜱᴜꜱ, ꜱᴏ ᴛʜᴀᴛ ᴛʜᴇ ʟɪꜰᴇ ᴏꜰ Jᴇꜱᴜꜱ ᴍᴀʏ ᴀʟꜱᴏ ʙᴇ ᴍᴀᴅᴇ ᴠɪꜱɪʙʟᴇ ɪɴ ᴏᴜʀ ʙᴏᴅɪᴇꜱ.

—2 Cᴏʀ. 4:7-10

we are more like Mary, we may meet God in Christ in the eyes, the voice, the physical touch of the person with a disabling condition. On the other hand, the person with a disabling condition may witness the love of Christ in being among a people in which one can laugh and cry, embrace and dance, or listen to music with a friend, and the promise of rest can be healing.

To teach a congregation to be with the person with a disabling condition is akin to Annie Dillard's essay "Teaching a Stone to Talk." At first, like teaching a stone to talk, a congregation will think we are daft in learning to just *be with* the one with a disability. For the person with a disability may be as sour in disposition as John could get sometimes, or may be disabled in such a way that communication may be nearly, or totally, impossible. The key? The practice of presence; of constancy, perseverance, or self-control in keeping company with one another, no matter how awkward it is to be with one another at first, second, or fourteenth glance. This is why it is easier to be like Martha than Mary: because one *looks* as if there is more work being done in the short term, although the real measure of God's grace is in Mary's posture, listening with her whole life to Jesus. Either by practice, or by God's grace, we will come to learn the richly intricate and always changing ways of being with each other, thus capable of enjoying one another's company more fully, having chosen, like Mary, the better part, which will not be taken away from her or us—being with the Lord and Savior of creation. For such is the kingdom of heaven.

Study Questions

1. Name at least one way that you or members of your congregation act more like "Martha" in welcoming people with disabilities into the church.

2. Name at least one way that you or members of your congregation act more like "Mary" in welcoming people with disabilities into the church.

Additional Resources

Black, Kathy. *A Healing Homiletic, Preaching and Disability.* Nashville: Abingdon Press, 1996.

Eiesland, Nancy L. *The Disabled God: Toward a Liberatory Theology of Disability.* Nashville: Abingdon Press, 1994.

Merrick, Lewis H. *And Show Steadfast Love: A Theological Look at Grace, Hospitality, Disabilities and the Church.* Louisville: Westminster/John Knox Press, 1993.

Webb-Mitchell, Brett. *Unexpected Guests at God's Banquet: Welcoming People with Disabilities into the Church.* New York: Crossroad, 1994.

8

Resources of the Presbyterian Church (U.S.A.)

Programs

Annual Retreat for Persons with Disabilities

For well over a dozen years, the Synod of the Trinity has hosted an annual retreat for persons with disabilities that could be a model program for other synods. Retired staff person Ray Brugler says that the retreat is open to all persons with disabilities from any denomination. "Up to seventy people can be accommodated in the completely accessible facilities at a conference center operated by the Church of the Brethren in the wooded hills of South-Central Pennsylvania."

The heavily advertised retreat is a three-day weekend that includes study and reflection led by a speaker, worship, recreation (even boating), crafts, and fellowship. Ray Brugler

LYDIA GANS

says, "A design team of twelve persons, both able and disabled, serving in rotating three-year terms, plans the retreat." In 1997, the program centered on the Scriptures and the music of jazz composer Dave Brubeck, and explored the life of Christ from his birth to the crucifixion and the resurrection. A subsidy for the event is budgeted each year in the synod's budget. Other costs are offset by participants' fees. For information, contact: Synod of the Trinity, Education, Vocation, and Nurture Unit, 3040 Market St., Camp Hill, PA 17011. Phone: (717) 737-0421; fax: (717) 737-8211; e-mail: syn.trinity@pcusa.org

Ghost Ranch Programs

For over a decade, this Presbyterian Church-run conference center has taken seriously the task of becoming accessible to persons with disabilities. It has sponsored a series of workshops significant to anyone interested in disability. For a program schedule or additional information contact: Ghost Ranch, HC 77 Box 11, Abiquiu, NM 87510; phone: (505) 685-4333.

Services and Resources

Office of Health Ministries

The 1988 General Assembly called churches to be congregations that encourage and promote health and wholeness. The Office of Health Ministries, a division of the National Ministries Division, Presbyterian Church (U.S.A.), assists Presbyterians, congregations, and governing bodies in responding to that call. It provides awareness education, direct services, and advocacy for equitable and just health care for all persons. Resources related to health and wholeness, alcohol and drug awareness, mental illness, and HIV/AIDS are produced by this office.

Presbyterian Parish Nursing is an important ministry of the Office of Health Ministries. The Parish Nurse program increases awareness of health-related issues, health education and

Enlarge the site of your tent, and let the curtains of your habitations be stretched out; do not hold back; lengthen your cords and strengthen your stakes.

—Isa. 54:2

counseling, pastoral care, referral, and advocacy at the parish level. For more information about the resources and services offered, call (502) 569-8100; or write: Office of Health Ministries, U.S.A., 100 Witherspoon St., Rm 3041B, Louisville, KY 40202-1396.

Presbyterian Health, Education, and Welfare Association (PHEWA)

PHEWA is a ministry of the National Ministries Division, Presbyterian Church (U.S.A.). It is a voluntary membership organization that provides resources for Presbyterians involved in social welfare and justice ministries. Divisions, or networks, within the organization specific to disability include Presbyterians for Disabilities Concerns (PDC), Presbyterian AIDS Network (PAN), Presbyterian Serious Mental Illness Network (PSMIN), Presbyterian Health Network (PHN), and Presbyterian Network on Alcohol and Other Drug Abuse (PNAODA). Membership benefits include regular newsletters and legislative alerts, networking and support, on-site consultations, and program development and evaluation. Publications, videos, and study materials produced by and specific to the ministry of each network are available for congregational education either free or at a nominal fee. A complete listing of these resources is available in the *PHEWA Resource Catalog*. For a copy of the resource catalog and membership information, contact: PHEWA, 100 Witherspoon St., Louisville, KY 40202; phone: (502) 569-5800; fax: (502) 569-8034.

PresbyNet

PresbyNet is an on-line computer service of the Office of Communication of the PC(USA) which frequently has information and electronic "meetings" pertinent to disability, as well as general church information. To access the PresbyNet system, you will need a computer, a modem, and software that runs on your computer modem and uses your modem. PresbyNet has a Starter Kit (ranging in price from $49.95 to $74.95, depending on your hardware requirements), which includes a special off-line reader that saves money by letting you read or write before you connect. For information or to order a Starter Kit, contact: PresbyNet, 100 Witherspoon St., Louisville, KY 40202-1396; phone: (502) 569-5138; e-mail: presbynet@pcusa.org

PresbyTel

PresbyTel is the toll-free information service of the PC(USA). Anyone can call and request information from databases of information on topics of concern to Presbyterians. Contact: 1-800-872-3283 (voice), 1-800-833-5988 (TDD); fax: (502) 569-8099; e-mail: presbytel@pcusa.org

Publications

Presbyterian Panel Report, Disabilities Issues, November 1993, is published by Research Services, Congregational Ministries Division, PC(USA), 100 Witherspoon St., Louisville, KY 40202. $5.00. DMS #70-360-94-201 (1-800-524-2612). The questionnaire was devoted to disabilities-related issues within the church.

Alternative Media

The following resources are currently available from the Presbyterian Publishing Corporation at 100 Witherspoon St., Louisville, KY 40202-1396. Call 1-800-227-2872 to inquire about discounts:

The Presbyterian Hymnal—Large Print Edition.
    Words only, no music. $15.95. Order PPC #01009880.

NRSV Companion Bible to the Presbyterian Hymnal—Large Print Edition.
    Pew edition Bible. $15.99. Order PPC #31090207.

The following resources are currently available from the National Braille Association, 3 Townline Circle, Rochester, NY 14623-2513; phone: (716) 427-8260.

The Presbyterian Hymnal—Braille Edition.
    18 volumes. For churches, the cost is $603.45; for individuals, $201.15. Binding is an additional $1 per volume.

The following resources for religious materials in large print and tape are available (contact each for their catalog or book list):

American Printing House for the Blind
    1839 Frankfort Ave.
    Louisville, KY 40206
    Toll-free: 1-800-223-1839

John Knox Tape Library
    John Knox Presbyterian Church
    109 S.W. Normandy Rd.
    Seattle, WA 98166
    Phone: (206) 241-1606

John Milton Society for the Blind
    475 Riverside Drive, Rm 455
    New York, NY 10115
    Phone: (212) 870-3335

Lutheran Braille Workers, Inc.
    P.O. Box 5000
    Yucapia, CA 92399
    Phone: (714) 795-8977

Lutheran Library for the Blind
    3558 South Jefferson Ave.
    St. Louis, MO 63118
    Phone: (402) 488-0981

9

Presbyterian Church (U.S.A.)
Contacts and Resources by Synod

Presbyterians throughout our synods have gifts and skills to offer those of us who are looking for information about disability. Although particular contacts may be identified as having a specialty, many also have a broad base of knowledge in access and disability to share with churches.

Synod of Alaska/Northwest

Presbytery of Seattle

Dorothy Gill, Disabilities Chairman
Woodland Park Presbyterian Church
   8015 Greenwood Ave. North
   Seattle, WA 98103
   Phone: (206) 782-1383

Woodland Park Presbyterian Church
   225 North 70th St.
   Seattle, WA 98103
   Phone: (206) 782-3776

In our church, we have several people who have had strokes. Two use wheelchairs, several use canes. We are on a level, with a lift going to the upper room (social hall). We have a braille copy of the *Book of Order* and we also now have several large-print hymnals.

Synod of the Covenant

Presbytery of Cincinnati

Kathleen Deyer Bolduc
   822 Carini Lane
   Cincinnati, OH 45218
   Phone: (513) 825-9319
   E-mail: Katebolduc@worldnet.att.net

I am the mother of three sons, one of whom has moderate mental retardation and autistic tendencies. I have a master of arts in religious studies. As a part of my degree work, I researched the impact of a child's disability on the family system. The outcome of that research was a handbook for churches titled *A Place Called Acceptance: Ministry with Families of Children with Disabilities* (see chapter 3 of this guide).

Presbytery of Detroit

Rev. David W. Robertson
   5171 Commerce Rd.
   Orchard Lake, MI 48324
   Phone: (248) 682-0730
   Fax: (248) 682-1718

We have recently made our church almost completely accessible. I have served on boards of agencies serving physically and mentally challenged persons.

Presbytery of Eastminster

John D. Sharick, Executive Presbyter
   Eastminster Presbytery
   45 Idlewood Rd., Ste. A
   Youngstown, OH 44515
   Phone: (330) 793-2416

E-mail: Eastmin@aol.com

Can provide churches' and pastors' names who have moved accessibility concerns through politics of congregations for new construction of facilities, and so forth.

Rev. William M. Youngblood
First Presbyterian Church
256 Mahonig Ave., N.W.
Warren, OH 44483
Phone: (330) 393-1524
E-mail: fpc@netdotcom.com

As part of a recent capital improvement project, a new ramp was installed into our building, along with an elevator, chair lift, and barrier-free rest room, making our facility fully barrier-free.

Presbytery of Lake Michigan

Fred B. Cunningham
North Presbyterian Church
603 N. Burdick St.
Kalamazoo, MI 49007
Phone: (616) 345-1848
E-mail: Flunning@net-link.net

For nine years North Presbyterian Church has had a special ministry with people who have a chronic and persistent mental illness. One-half of our eighty parishioners are people with a mental illness and are integrated into the total life of the church. We also sponsor a weekly activity group for people of the church and community who have a mental illness. Eighty people are called each week for the activity.

Presbytery of Mackinac

Barbara H. Robbins
P.O. Box 13
Iron River, MI 49935
Phone: (906)265-4865
Fax: (906) 265-5605
E-mail: brobbins@up.net

I've worn hearing aids for thirty years. I've introduced sign language to hearing kids for twenty years. . . . I serve on the board of directors of Outdoors Forever and worked to see that state parks have TTYs installed. I attend First Presbyterian Church of Iron River, Michigan, where the pastor provides a copy of the sermon before the service so I can follow along.

Presbytery of Scioto Valley

Sandra R. Byers, Ph.D., R.N.
Worthington Presbyterian Church
773 High St.
Worthington, OH 43085
Phone: (614) 885-5355
Fax: (614) 885-3101

Our church has removed pews to accommodate wheelchairs. We have installed an elevator in a new section.

Catherine R. Hare, Educator
Amesville-New England Parish
P.O. Box 159
Amesville, OH 45711
Phone: (740) 448-6401

Our parish has for the past twenty-five years sponsored a program that runs from the first Thursday in October through the first Thursday in May. The program is held at the Athens First Presbyterian Church. Our program is for people with mental retardation, and includes twenty-five to thirty school age children and adults each month. Along with those persons with disabilities who attend the program, there are ten to fifteen program facilitators, as well as several children of those program facilitators. I have a master's degree in education (major: special education) and taught in a school for children with disabilities for twenty-four years. Our program lets all attending know what the love of Jesus is like. In this church, there is an elevator.

Rev. Kay Dawson Puckett
26376 Legion Rd.
Langsville, OH 45741
Phone: (740) 669-7441
E-mail: Kay_Puckett.parti@ecunet.org

As a pew person and pastor, I have become increasingly aware of those who have what I now call invisible or hidden disabilities. Many persons in our churches with hidden physical or emotional limitations appear healthy but are not able to fully participate in activities or worship. I am now one of those persons with hidden disabilities that prevent me from working and allow very little activity away from home. I hope to be able to help, as churches minister more wholly with those of us with hidden disabilities.

Lois A. Simms
155 W. Main St. #705
Columbus, OH 43215
Phone: (614) 228-3820
Broad Street Presbyterian Church
760 E. Broad Street
Columbus, OH 43205
Phone: (614) 221-6552

I have a disability—use a wheelchair, and so forth. My church is accessible. We have just cut out a pew for wheelchairs. It has been accessible for years, except for the pews.

Presbytery of the Western Reserve

Rev. Mark Koenig, Co-pastor
Noble Road Presbyterian Church
2780 Noble Rd.
Cleveland Heights, OH 44121
Phone: (216) 382-0660
E-mail: nobleroad@juno.com

Our congregation has begun to explore the possibilities of ministry with people who are deaf. Two members, one who is deaf and one who is hearing, taught a class in signed English. Our Easter and Pentecost worship services were interpreted into sign. Portions of the service are interpreted into sign on a weekly basis.

The Rev. Ms. Jody C. Lefort
Fairmount Presbyterian Church
2757 Fairmount Blvd.
Cleveland Heights, OH 44118
Phone: (216) 321-5800
Fax: (216) 321-1044
E-mail: jlefort@fairmount church.org

I am a pastor with responsibilities for educational ministry. The congregation I serve has a long history of responding to the needs of children with special needs. Because each situation is different, what I can share is more a process of awareness and response than a written curriculum resource.

Synod of Lakes and Prairies

Presbytery of Des Moines

Pam Avaux, Coordinator of Lay Ministries
Westminster Presbyterian Church
4114 Allison Ave.
Des Moines, IA 50310-3398
Phone: (515) 274-1534
Fax: 515-274-1537
E-mail: Westpres@netins.net

We have offered an interpreter for the deaf and hearing impaired for Sunday worship and special services and for our fine arts programs. We have a wheelchair lift on our van. We have an elevator entrance with braille signs. We provide wheelchairs at our accessible entrances. We are undergoing a building renovation in hopes of equipping for disabilities.

Presbytery of East Iowa

Rev. Mark W. Martin
St. Andrew Presbyterian Church
1300 Melrose Ave.
Iowa City, IA 52246
Phone: (319) 338-7523
Fax: (319) 338-8599
E-mail: therev@inav.net

St. Andrew is completely accessible to persons with disabilities. I have worked with several disabled persons in this congregation over the past eleven years, but do not consider myself as a person with particular expertise in this area.

Presbytery of the Homestead

Raymond Meester, Pastor
Heritage Presbyterian Church
880 S. 35th St.
Lincoln, NE 68510-3499
Phone: (402) 477-3401
E-mail: heritage@inetnebr.com

My parents, as well as four uncles and aunts, are deaf. I am conversant in American Sign Language, knowledgeable about Deaf Culture, and am on the board of the Nebraska Commission for the Deaf and Hard of Hearing. The church I pastor currently has ten deaf members and four deaf children. Our worship service is interpreted into American Sign Language each Sunday. One deaf member serves on the session, and session meetings are interpreted. We have a TTY (telephone device for the deaf) with a dedicated phone line. Our church has invited various deaf community groups to use our facilities, and each year we host a Christmas party for local deaf children at which a "signing Santa" makes his appearance. Annually, we host a church interpreters' training workshop and a special "Deaf Sunday." The worship is led in American Sign Language and is voiced for the hearing, and a deaf pastor preaches. We are in the process of offering Christian education opportunities for the deaf children and plan to provide interpreters in the Sunday school classes of our deaf children. We also conduct sign language classes at the church.

Darlene Paul
6700 Flint Ridge
Lincoln, NE 68506
Phone: (402) 483-4366
E-mail: dpaul@unlinfo2.unl.edu

I am currently a sign language interpreter who works with a local church to include the deaf community in its worship services and provide support for their secular activities.

Presbytery of John Knox

Dr. Robert M. Healey
Eaglecrest Commons #32
2945 Lincoln Drive North
Roseville, MN 55113

I have a disability and initiated John Knox Presbytery's overture to General Assembly to list persons with disabilities among minorities that must be included as active participants in all phases of the life of the Presbyterian Church. I have advised Presbyteries' Cooperative Committees concerning standard ordination questions on the subject of including persons with disabilities. I continue to press for recognition of ease of handling as essential to any concept of "accessibility" (lever door handles, bulletins making hymnbooks unnecessary, etc).

Presbytery of Prospect Hill

Carol J. Johnson-Miller
P.O. Box 113
Estherville, IA 51334
Phone: (712) 362-5667
E-mail: Carol.Miller@estherville.k12.ia.us
First Presbyterian Church
723 First Avenue South
Estherville, IA 51334
Phone: (712) 362-4772

Carol has taught a Sunday church school class for persons with mental illness or mental retardation, which was started in her church, First Presbyterian, in 1982. Several members of the class have served as ushers. Carol can share curriculum ideas and other specifics about her church's program.

Synod of Lincoln Trails

Southeast Presbytery

Paul Rosenberger
356 Holiday Drive
Decatur, IL 62526
Phone: (217) 877-4789
First Presbyterian Church
204 West Prairie
Decatur, IL 62523
Phone: (217) 429-4195

I have used a wheelchair for fifteen years. Our church, First Presbyterian, has made many physical renovations to accommodate deaf, low-vision, and mobility limited persons. I have consulted on modifications and have conducted ADA inspections for a center for independent living. I am a state board member for the Coalition of Citizens with Disabilities in Illinois.

Synod of Living Waters

Louisville Presbytery

Evelyn Byrd
7414 Woodhill Valley Rd.
Louisville, KY 40241
Phone: (502) 228-8840
E-mail: byrdbliss@juno.com

I have been a community advocate for persons (all ages) with mental retardation for more than thirty years. Calvin Presbyterian Church (where I am an elder) has given space for four years for a day activity program for mentally handicapped adults, called Partnerships. Also, the Presbyterian camp, Cedar Ridge Camp, offers mentally retarded children the opportunity to participate in the summer camping events. I was a part of the planning of this. . . . Calvin Presbyterian Church hosts the annual picnic for the Council for Retarded Citizens of Jefferson County.

Rev. Kenneth J. Hockenberry
Beulah Presbyterian Church
6704 Bardstown Rd.
Louisville, KY 40291
Phone: (502) 239-3231
E-mail: Ken_Hockenberry.parti@pcusa.org

The congregation I serve has six active members who use wheelchairs, and we have made great gains in accessibility matters here at Beulah, including accessible automatic doors, and ramps (which everyone uses). We are currently (1998–1999) redesigning our chancel area for this purpose.

Jim Krauss-Jackson, M. Div., M. Ed.
127 Bonner Ave.
Louisville, KY 40207
Phone: (502) 896-0426
E-mail: Jane_Krauss_Jackson@pcusa.org

I am a retired minister attending a church that has included ramps, handicapped parking areas, an elevator, and spaces for wheelchairs in the sanctuary. The building is accessible for wheelchairs, except the choir loft. I had a knee replacement in 1997 and experienced using a walker and cane. My expertise is in working with those having mental illness, often not included in disability lists.

North Alabama Presbytery

Tom Maynor, Ed.D.
1011 A. Prospect Dr., S.E.
Decatur, AL 35601
Phone: (256) 353-0253
E-mail: ssilmon@hiWaay.net
First Presbyterian Church
701 Oak Street, NE
Decatur, AL 35601
Phone: (256) 353-0253
Fax: (256) 353-0377

I am the supervisor of developmental programs for the Decatur city schools. The staff and I saw a need to provide our students with community experiences. First Presbyterian, Westminster Presbyterian Church, and Wesley Memorial United Methodist Church were asked to provide their facilities and personnel to assist us. They opened their doors to provide training environments and other opportunities for students from Decatur high school's developmental program for students with mental disabilities. Tasks are tailored to the student's abilities. Beyond the acquisition of work skills, the students are provided an opportunity to practice communication and social skills with people they encounter while on the job.

Ministers, office staff, custodians, and members of the respective congregations have an opportunity to become actively engaged in the growth and development of these special young people. This partnership provides opportunities for churches to have a need met while assisting a public school in the accomplishment of its mission.

Synod of Mid-America

Giddings Lovejoy

Becky Valicott, Parish Nurse
Tyler Presbyterian Church
2109 South Spring Ave.
St. Louis, MO 63123
Phone: (314) 772-1317
Fax: (314) 772-4283

I am a parish nurse at Tyler Place Presbyterian Church where we have installed an approved ramp, an elevator, and handicapped-accessible rest rooms. Our sanctuary has theater-type seating, and we have recently decided to remove two seats on each side of the seating area to accommodate wheelchairs or higher-seat chairs with arms. The parish nurse is also available for individual assessments and consultations.

Heartland Presbytery

Marty Lynch, Director of Special Ministries
Colonial Presbyterian Church
95 and Warnall
Kansas City, MO 64114
Phone: (816) 942-3272
Fax: (816) 942-8032

Colonial Presbyterian Church has established an outreach to persons with special needs, called Special Ministries. This ministry now has a full-time staff person and many volunteers to organize its programs. The program began twelve years ago with Abounding Love, an outreach to persons with developmental disabilities. This includes Sunday school classes; evening programs for spiritual growth and recreation; and parent support groups. This program ministers to over one hundred young people and their parents. Another program, Care 'n Club, is for adults with long-term mental illness but living in the community. We meet weekly to have a Bible study, pray, and support each other. A deaf outreach is now being established. We are giving weekly mini-workshops to prepare the congregation, and have a goal of interpreting all services and increasing outreach to the deaf. We will be glad to respond to anyone wanting to start a special ministry and to share in how to build a program.

Presbytery of Southern Kansas

Rev. Skip Johnson
Northminster Presbyterian Church
1100 W. 21st
Hutchinson, KS 67502
Phone: (316) 662-9439
E-mail: Skipjohnson@mindsprint.com

Several members of our church were instrumental in founding Hutchinson

Heights, which is a residential home for adults with severe physical disabilities. We have intentionally made the original building and the new addition accessible. Several residents of the Heights are members of our church and two are currently deacons. All our church-related activities have included the Heights residents, and in 1999 we will be joined on our annual intergenerational snow-skiing trip by several of the Heights residents.

Synod of Mid-Atlantic

Charlotte Presbytery

Priscilla B. Durkin, Pastor
First Presbyterian Church
208 Greene St.
Wadesboro, NC 28170
Phone: (704) 694-3818 (church);
(704) 694-9869 (home)

We have installed a lift and removed pews to create space for wheelchairs. We will budget an audio system so that those with hearing impairments may individually control the volume of the worship leaders.

James Presbytery

Rev. Norman D. Nettleton
142 West Park Drive
Charlottesville, VA 22901-2504
Phone: (804) 296-3295
E-mail: 104077.1143@compuserve.com

I am a person with a disability that affects the use of my entire right side. I have had this disability for the entire time of my pastoral ministry which has extended for over fifty years. In recent years I attended a workshop on disability issues at Ghost Ranch in New Mexico, a conference center of the Presbyterian Church (U.S.A.), and received valuable information concerning myself and other persons with disabilities as well as what churches may be doing to welcome and involve persons with disabilities. I have been instrumental in the inclusion of disability issues in the structure of presbytery organization.

New Hope Presbytery

Robert W. Owens, Coordinator
State of North Carolina,
    Department of Administration
Office on the Americans with Disabilities Act
217 West Jones St.
Raleigh, NC 27603-1336
Phone: (919) 715-2302
Fax: (919) 733-9571

I am a person who has a mobility impairment. I walk with crutches. Also, I have worked professionally in the area of disabilities for twenty-eight years. Presently, I am coordinator of the North Carolina Office on the Americans with Disabilities Act. I am also a Presbyterian elder, not currently on session.

Synod of the Northeast

Albany Presbytery

Marriellen Boomhower, Property Chair
    12 Compton Place
    Scotia, NY 12302
    Phone: (518) 399-1694
    E-mail: mboomho155@aol.com
Trinity Presbyterian Church
    185 Swaggertown Rd.
    Scotia, NY 12302
    Phone: (518) 399-8782

I led a group at our small church (130 members) to make our building accessible to all. We raised almost $17,000 to build a concrete ramp into the church, installed a new sound system, and created a unisex accessible bathroom in what was formerly a storage area. I have developed a file of ADA requirements and federal, state, and local regulations. I also have addresses and phone numbers of agencies and contractors who have specialized knowledge in this area. This project began as a few individuals' dream and eventually bloomed into a reality that involved everyone in the church in some capacity.

Boston Presbytery

Ann Madsen Dailey, Speech/Language
    Pathologist
10 Mill St., Unit N
Maynard, MA 01754
Phone: (978) 897-7428
E-mail: Amdailey@aol.com

My church in Sudbury (the Presbyterian church) has an interpreter for a deaf child. He is now in college and worships with us when he is home, but the church started this program when he was in middle school. A course was provided for the children in his church school class to learn sign. The course was open to anyone in the church and the community at large (for a reasonable fee to nonmembers). This is the only need that has arisen within my church, other than making it accessible.

Elizabeth Presbytery

Judith Wussler, Preschool-Primary Coordinator
Children's Specialized Hospital
    330 South Ave.
    Fanwood, NJ 07023
    Phone: (908) 301-2528
    Fax: (908) 301-2517

I've worked in a hospital-based private school for children with developmental delays for twenty years. Our family provided foster care, for a time, for a (now) young woman, and we remain close friends with her and her family. I was instrumental in initiating the building of a wheelchair access ramp at the front of my church. I am a member of the New Jersey Coalition for Inclusive Ministries.

Geneva Presbytery

Samuel L. Edwards, Executive Presbyter
Presbytery of Geneva
    89 Main St., P.O. Box 278
    Dresden, NY 14441
    Phone: (315) 536-7753
    Fax: (315) 536-2128

Presbyteries of Geneva and Genesee Valley sponsor camps for developmentally disabled youth and young adults at Camp Whitman on Seneca Lake in Dresden, New York. Contact the address above for more information.

Diane Wheeler
P.O. Box 55
Palmyra, NY 14522

Provided braille copies of presbytery meetings and other church-related publications for a blind pastor in another presbytery.

Long Island Presbytery

Norman W. Minard, D.Min.
57 Freemont Lane
Coram, NY 11727-3240
Phone: (516)732-6506

I am a retired Presbyterian minister and VA hospital chaplain. I was born with birth injuries and got polio at age three. For most of my life I have sought to be a role model for others with disabilities. I have been an advocate within my communities and the church. I am willing and able to help others to be advocates.

Northern New York Presbytery

Rev. William J. Richard, Jr.
1102 Tri-Town Road
Addison, VT 05491
Phone/Fax: (802) 759-2777

I was born with congenital glaucoma and have served the body of Christ by faith as member, church school student and teacher, youth fellowship participant, seminarian, and ordained minister in the Presbyterian Church (U.S.A.). My "pastures" have been small churches and, for twenty-four years, campus ministry. I have helped individuals and families in their struggles to transform blindness from an isolating condition into the sharing of their gifts through participation in the new community of love and empowerment that the risen Christ creates. The same goes for congregations and governing bodies who want to share in a ministry of partnership with persons with disabilities.

My activities in church affairs have been at all governing body levels, and include member, Leadership Team, Presbyterians for Disability Concerns a network of PHEWA; member, recently formed Commission on Enabling Ministry Services of the General Assembly; member, Synod of the Trinity committee that initiated annual retreats for persons in churches with disabilities. Please let me know if I can be of help in consultation.

Presbytery of Southern New England

Charles W. Watt
8 Lord Place
Old Saybrook, CT 06475-2107
Phone: (860) 388-9449
E-mail: Chuck.Watt@pcusa.org

As presbytery and General Assembly staff, before I retired, I worked with churches and task forces to improve access for persons with handicapping conditions. More recently, limitations have made it necessary for me to use the disability requirements to meet my own needs. I'm happy to consult with persons working to meet practical problems of making the church accessible, as well as those who advocate with disabled persons.

Presbytery of Western New York

Susan Earle, Elder
Hamburg Presbyterian Church
177 Main St.
Hamburg, NY 14075
Phone: (716) 649-1970
Fax: (716) 649-1971
E-mail: HPC@pcom.net

I am a parent of an adult son with brain damage. I have experience helping my church develop a monthly worship service for residents in group homes. This service takes place in the church chapel.

Synod of the Pacific

Sacramento Presbytery

The Rev. Timothy H. Little, D. Min., Chair
IDAP (Interfaith Disability Awareness Project)
4135 Los Coches Way
Sacramento, CA 95864
Phone: (916) 972-1942
E-mail: slittle@unidial.com

IDAP was established in 1996 to celebrate the gifts and talents of persons with disabilities in the faith communities of Greater Sacramento. Its annual conference and celebration of Disability Awareness Sabbath are designed to encourage congregations to engage in disability audits. In addition, the Rev. Dr. Timothy H. Little (chaplain and clinical pastoral education supervisor at UCD Medical Center, legally blind from birth and totally blind since 1992), and Sandra Little, MFCC therapist, have designed and presented a workshop and adult church school curriculum to encourage adults and youth to explore what it feels like to receive a disability. This workshop recognizes that architectural and communication barriers may often be more obvious, but breaking down resistance to change depends on changes in attitudinal barriers.

San Francisco Presbytery

Rev. Jeff Gaines
Seventh Avenue Presbyterian Church
  1329 Seventh Ave.
  San Francisco, CA 94122-2507
  Phone: (415) 664-2543
  Fax: (415)664-4017
  E-mail: JGAINES@sdiworld.org

Our church (main floor) is accessible. We have two members (who use) wheelchairs, as does one parish associate. We've reconfigured the pews, allowing spaces where folks in wheelchairs can choose to sit. Our goal is to work on making the second floor accessible as well. This goal is dependent on a grant: We need an elevator.

San Joaquin Presbytery

Lu Ann Ruoss, Dir. Special Needs Ministries
First Presbyterian Church
  1705 17th St.
  Bakersfield, CA 93301
  Phone: (805) 325-9419
  Fax: (805) 325-9419

I have several family members with disabilities, some physical and some developmental. I have been developing a ministry with adults with developmental disabilities here at our church and in the community. This ministry addresses the need for spiritual growth and finding areas

of service within the body of Christ appropriate to the individual's gifts. I have developed ways of adapting different materials for different learners so various levels of ability can participate together. I established Access Sunday as a yearly event at our church to provide information and increase awareness about people with disabilities and their abilities. First Presbyterian is working at removing barriers within our congregation. Because of a van with a lift that has been donated recently, we are able to provide some transportation, as well as having assisted listening devices, large-print bulletins, and audiotapes of the sermons. We have access to braille material and signers, if needed. I would share any information gained through this process and encourage networking with others interested.

Stockton Presbytery

John Russell-Curry
c/o Sierra Presbyterian Church
  P.O. Box 656
  Merced, CA 95340
  Phone: (209) 383-6662
  E-mail: jrussel@mcoe.merced.k12.ca.us

I am a tent-making pastor who works with students and families with severe physical impairments. I have also worked with the developmentally disabled and emotionally disturbed. Our church also houses a center for independent living and is available for numerous support groups for the disabled. We always print a large-print version of our bulletin. We are being considered to house a program for severely disabled college students. In addition, I am president of the local Cerebral Palsy Association.

Synod of Rocky Mountains

Pueblo Presbytery

North Presbyterian Church
Rev. Franklin Medford
  3025 West 37th Ave.
  Denver, CO 80211
  Phone: (303) 433-7131

North Presbyterian has a number of persons with disabilities who attend and are active members.

Westminster Presbyterian Church
Rev. Henry O. Hanna
  10 University Circle
  Pueblo, CO 81005
  Phone: (719) 561-8031

Westminster Presbyterian is a barrier-free church with a tape ministry for persons who can no longer attend worship. Westminster also has large-print bulletins and hymnals. Amplifiers are available for persons who are hard of hearing.

Synod of South Atlantic

Central Florida Presbytery

Joyce P. Davis, Director of Resident Care
The Duvall Home
  3395 Grand Ave.
  P.O. Box 220036
  Glenwood, FL 32722
  Phone: (904) 734-2874
  Fax: (904) 734-5504
  E-mail: duvall@intersrv.com

The Duvall Home is a twenty-four hour residential care facility for the mentally retarded. The home (a nonprofit organization operated by the Presbyterian Special Services, Inc., in relationship with the Presbyterian Church (U.S.A.)) was established and exists for the benefit of children and adults who by reason of mental retardation require partial or total care. The Duvall Home seeks to provide the highest quality of life and greatest possible level of independence for each resident within the context of a family home.

Charleston-Atlantic Presbytery

Mrs. Jean D. May
Presbyterian Home, CMR 163
  201 W. 9th North St.
  Summerville, SC 29483

  Mt. Pleasant Church, Mt. Pleasant, South Carolina (home church), has built a ramp (other churches in the area have too),

installed hearing devices, large-print hymnals, handrails, elevators, and so on. Presbyterian Homes of South Carolina has made sure any new construction is accessible.

Greater Atlanta Presbytery

Peter Marshall
Mt. Vernon Presbyterian Church
  471 Mt. Vernon Hwy., N.E.
  Atlanta, GA 30328
  Phone: (404) 255-2211
  Fax: (404) 255-4619
  E-mail: MTVERNONPRES@worldnet.att.net

Maggie Eanes
Roswell Presbyterian Church
  755 Mimosa Blvd.
  Roswell, GA 30075-4407
  Phone: (770) 993-6316
  Fax: (770) 993-6472
  E-mail: Roswell@aol.com

My (Peter's) experience has been as a licensed social worker in hospitals for twenty-five years and I am also a physically challenged person. Mt. Vernon Presbyterian Church in Atlanta and Roswell Presbyterian Church in Roswell, Georgia, have been supportive and encouraging in starting Project Faith Disability Outreach Ministry that can be duplicated in other churches. We have the disabled become part of our ministry to others. Disability committees are starting in both churches and they are adhering to the National Organization on Disability (regarding) establishment of disability certification.

Synod of Southern California and Hawaii

Los Ranchos Presbytery

Rev. Robert Pietsch
Trinity Presbyterian Church
  13922 Prospect Ave.
  Santa Ana, CA 92705
  Phone: (714) 544-7850

Parent of a child with developmental disabilities who died at age twenty-seven;

doctoral dissertation on the Church and Disabilities Ministry from San Francisco Theological Seminary; executive director of ministry that assisted churches in developing ministry with persons with disabilities from 1987 to 1995 (in Southern California); served on National Council of Churches Committee on Disabilities; taught various seminars on disability awareness and inclusion; and developed ministry at Trinity Presbyterian over past twenty-five years, with a strong emphasis on inclusion.

Synod of the Southwest

Grand Canyon Presbytery

Ms. Anne R. McAllister, Elder
38925 E. Roma Ave.
Phoenix, AZ 85018
Phone: (602) 955-4196
Palo Cristi Presbyterian Church
3535 E. Lincoln Drive
Paradise Valley, AZ 5253
Phone: (602) 955-6080
Fax: (602) 955-8729

Having a hearing disability myself, I serve on the Task Force for Inclusiveness at Palo Cristi Presbyterian Church. The sanctuary has been equipped with a new, upgraded sound system, with hearing sets available on request for additional amplification. The church recently purchased a hand-held microphone that can be used for group discussions, such as sermon afterthoughts or study sessions. This permits everyone to hear and participate comfortably.

Santa Fe Presbytery

S. David Jennings, Deacon
1525 Tomasita St., N.E.
Albuquerque, NM 87112-4449
Phone: (505) 294-4605
First Presbyterian Church
215 Locust St., N.E.
Albuquerque, NM 87102
Phone: (505) 247-9593

I am available as a resource person with extensive files of training and sensitivity materials and resources assembled by the late Nancy G. Jennings (a former moderator of Presbyterians for Disabilities Concerns) and supplements with new materials assembled since her death. Our church, First Presbyterian, makes considerable effort to accommodate handicapped members with ramps and elevator (original to 1955 building), handicapped parking (enlarged twice in the past five years), accessible rest rooms (upgraded in 1997), large-print bulletins and hymnals, FM loop hearing aids, audio- and videotape ministry available every Sunday as requested, and stair lift installed in 1996 in Westminster House (adjacent social/educational structure).

Synod of the Sun

Arkansas Presbytery

Michael Harper, Director of Youth Ministries
600 Pleasant Valley Drive
Little Rock, AR 72227
Phone: (501) 227-0000
Fax: (501) 227-6117

I am a youth director who has a junior high adviser (adult) in a wheelchair. We have learned how to plan inclusive activities for youth and adults. With her positive presence in our group, our youth have become sensitive to people with special needs. This is especially true on ski trips and camping trips.

Grace Presbytery

Rev. Peggy Stoll Schave, Chaplain
10601 Parkfield
Austin, TX 78758
Phone: (512) 837-8957

I was a chaplain at a mental institution for two years. I was a chaplain at a state school for persons with profound and severe mental retardation for three years. Now I'm working with persons who have had brain injuries, persons who are dying (hospice, Austin), and persons in crisis (on-call chaplain at acute-care hospitals). I've also done presentations at clinical pastoral education groups, local churches, and a seminary on ministry with persons with mental illness and mental retardation.

Mission Presbytery

Rev. Linda Reinhardt
The Jeremiah Project
222 Soft Wind
Canyon Lake, TX 78133-9701
Phone: (830) 935-4618

I am the pastor of a church and the director of a ministry that serves people with environmental-toxin–induced illnesses, such as chemical sensitivity, chronic fatigue, sick building syndrome, fibromyalgia, silicone breast implant illnesses, and Gulf War Syndrome. I am disabled from a pesticide poisoning in 1987. The Jeremiah Project has a resource library with over five thousand articles, studies, and documents regarding environmental toxins and human health, which we make available to ministers, churches, and individuals nationwide.

Richard S. Robertson, President
Westminster Environmental Illness Corp.
3208 Exposition Blvd.
Austin, TX 78703
Phone: (512) 453-7174
E-mail: rsr@onr.com

Westminster Presbyterian Church in Austin formed a nonprofit corporation out of the session to minister to persons suffering from MCS (Multiple Chemical Sensitivity). We bought 1.5 acres of land and an old mobile home, dug a well and septic system, brought in electricity and telephone, and are in the process of rebuilding the mobile home after stripping it to the walls and redesigning the interior. All of the building involves using safe building materials that (persons with MCS) can tolerate.

We have moved a woman (a member of the church) and her old Morgan Building (which our church bought thirteen years ago) to the site prior to completion of the project. She has had MCS for many years and is considered disabled by the government, as she is on SSI. She tries to support herself by weaving and is a very accomplished weaver. Part of the refurbished mobile home will have space for her studio.

Synod of the Trinity

Philadelphia Presbytery

Calvin E. Uzelmeier, Jr.
Warminster Church
500 Madison Ave.
Warminster, PA 18974
Phone: (215) 675-0801
Fax: (215) 675-0812
E-mail: warmpres@aol.com

Warminster Church has been reaching people with disabilities since 1975. Alterations to bathrooms were made economically. Programs are offered for all types of disabilities, including signing for the hearing impaired, signing choir, special education church school class; large-print hymnbooks, Bibles, and church bulletins; one-month summer day camp for severely mentally impaired, and hospital equipment available for loan.

Nancy J. Unks
608 E. Valley Green Rd.
Flourtown, PA 19031
Phone: (215) 233-5825
E-mail: unks@bellatlantic.net

I am the wife of a severely disabled individual who is unable to move or speak. Our church helped to raise the money to purchase the Eyegaze Computer System that enables him to communicate. Areas of expertise I would be happy to share with individuals or churches include accessibility issues, communicating with those who cannot talk, managing daily caregiving, and supporting long-term primary caregivers.

Pittsburgh Presbytery

Rev. Jean H. Henderson
The Presbyterian Church
414 Grant St.
Sewickley, PA 15143
Phone: (412) 741-4550
Fax: (412) 41-1210

The Presbyterian Church has a functioning Disabilities Issues Committee (meets monthly), an annual Presbyterian Access Sunday with speakers, an elevator and two ramps (outside), and a large amount of medical equipment for loan; supplies hearing devices and large-print bulletins for worship; sponsors a group for young adults with disabilities which meets semimonthly; and I have served as an advocate for DMS service on local public TV.

Shenango Presbytery

The Rev. Dr. Ray B. Brugler
2971 Melvin Drive
New Castle, PA 16105-1622
Phone: (724) 658-6289
E-mail: rbpb@shenango.org

Ray is the former staff person (now retired) for the Synod of the Trinity's annual retreat for persons with disabilities and can share information about how that program works.

Dawn Magaro, President
Compassionate Ministries
3040 Market St.
Camp Hill, PA 17011
Phone: (717) 730-9755
E-mail: atadmi@aol.com

I am a caregiver for several family members who have disabilities. Compassionate Ministries is a nonprofit organization that reaches out to all in the community to help with and establish a network of people-helping-people, filling the gap between social and health services.

Ann M. Osborne, Associate
Education, Vocation, and Nurture Unit
Synod of the Trinity
3040 Market St.
Camp Hill, PA 17011
Phone: (717) 737-0421
Fax: (717) 737-8211
E-mail: syn.trinity@pcusa.org

The Synod of the Trinity holds a Bible study retreat for persons with disabilities during the second weekend in September at a fully accessible retreat center in South Central Pennsylvania. The retreat is designed by and hosted by persons with disabilities and their care providers. It is ecumenical in nature, with seventy to eighty participants annually.

Sue S. Montgomery, Co-pastor, Chaplain
614 Elmwood Ave.
Grove City, PA 16127-1414
Phone: (724) 458-0843
E-mail: Trinitypar@shenango.org

I am a chaplain at a facility for persons with mental retardation. My ministry in the area of mental retardation and faith development is focused on serious to pervasive mental retardation. As a person with a mobility disability, I have been active in advocacy issues and theological issues and have led workshops on accessibility, welcoming persons with disabilities, and on the theology of disabilities.

West Virginia Presbytery

Mark Lampley, Associate Pastor for Christian Education
First Presbyterian Church
16 Broad St.
Charleston, WV 25301
Phone: (304) 343-3741
E-mail: RevLampley@aol.com

Our church has developed and been awarded outreach to (persons with mental impairments). We have a church school class and handbell group that utilizes more than thirty volunteers, including youth for work with the TMI group. The Rainbow church school class has been existing since the '70s. Our building, including elevators, rest rooms, ramps, and worship sites, is wheelchair accessible. We have plans for making public phones accessible to wheelchair levels as well as installing braille throughout the facilities.

Notes

Preface

1. Mary Jane Owen, "The Wisdom of Human Vulnerability," *The Disability Rag & Resource*, Vol. 14, No. 3 (May/June 1993): 19.

Introduction

These edited comments were provided as a handout for a workshop on the church and ADA at the Presbyterian Health, Education, and Welfare Association Biennial in 1995.

1. Johanna W. H. Bos, "A Wideness of Mercy," in *And Show Steadfast Love* (Louisville: Presbyterian Publishing House, 1993), p. 11.

2. Edward F. Campbell Jr., "Ruth," *The Anchor Bible* (Garden City, NY: Doubleday, 1975), p. 113.

1. Disability 101

1. Ginny Thornburgh, *Loving Justice: The ADA and the Religious Community* (Washington, D.C.: National Organization on Disability, 1994), p. 3. Used with permission.

2. From the *Minutes of the 203rd General Assembly (1991)* (Part 1) #32.041-6, p. 630.

3. Rev. Stella Dempski, from comments at a disability consultation with the Commission on Enabling Ministry Services in Louisville in November 1997.

4. Brett Webb-Mitchell, from comments at a disability consultation with the Commission on Enabling Ministry Services in Louisville, in November 1997.

5. Ann Rose Davies and Ginny Thornburgh, *That All May Worship: An Interfaith Welcome to People with Disabilities* (Washington, D.C.: National Organization on Disability, 1994), p. 11. Used with permission.

6. Barbara Ramnaraine and Mary Jane Steinhagen, *AccessAbility: A Manual for Churches* (St. Paul, MN.: Diocesan Office on Ministry with Persons Who Are Disabled of the Episcopal Diocese of Minnesota and Office for People with Disabilities, Catholic Charities of the Archdiocese of St. Paul, MN, 1997), p. 7. Reprinted with permission.

7. Adapted from guidelines in a brochure published by Paraquad, Inc., and the Research and Training Center on Independent Living, as cited in Ramnaraine and Steinhagen, *AccessAbility*, p. 7. Reprinted with permission.

2. Communication Access

1. Ann Rose Davis and Ginny Thornburgh, *That All May Worship: An Interfaith Welcome to People with Disabilities* (Washington, D.C.: National Organization on Disability, 1994), p. 25. Used with permission.

2. *A Guide to Planning Accessible Meetings* (Houston, TX: ILRU Research and Training Center on Independent Living, 1993), p. 38.

3. Ibid.

4. "Removing the Barriers to Communication," *Life & Times*, vol. xiv, no. 6 (Synod of Lakes and Prairies, 1997): 4.

5. *A Guide to Planning Accessible Meetings*, p. 42.

6. "What Is a Learning Disability?" *The Barnard/Columbia Women's Handbook 1992*, retrieved March 10, 1998, from the World Wide Web: http://www.columbia.edu:71/00/publications/women/wh42

7. Margot Hausmann, "Multisensory Worship Ideas," a list compiled by the author and reprinted with permission. Write to Chaplain Margot Hausmann, Eastern Christian Children's Retreat, 700 Mountain Ave., Wyckoff, NJ 07481.

3. Recognizing the Gifts of Persons with Developmental Disabilities, Mental Retardation, Mental Illness, and other Brain-based Illnesses

1. Ann Rose Davis and Ginny Thornburgh, *That All May Worship: An Interfaith Welcome to People with Disabilities* (Washington, D.C.: National Organization on Disability, 1994), p. 29. Used with permission.

2. Ibid., p. 27.

3. Barbara Ramnaraine and Mary Jane Steinhagen, *AccessAbility: A Manual for Churches* (St. Paul, MN: Diocesan Office on Ministry with Persons Who Are Disabled of the Episcopal Diocese of Minnesota and Office for People with Disabilities, Catholic Charities of the Archdiocese of St. Paul, MN, 1997), p. 44.

4. Including Persons with Hidden Disabilities

1. Ann Rose Davis and Ginny Thornburgh, *That All May Worship: An Interfaith Welcome to People with Disabilities* (Washington, D.C.: National Organization on Disability, 1994), p. 33. Used with permission.

5. Removing Architectural Barriers

1. Presbyterian Panel Report (Louisville: Research Services, Congregational Ministries Division, PC(USA), November 1993), pp. 5–6.

2. Building Accessibility loans from the Church Loan Program, PC(USA), can be made up to the total cost of the contractor's estimate, not to exceed $30,000, with an interest rate of 3 percent and maximum term of fifteen years. These loans may include, but are not limited to, ramps, elevators, accessible restrooms, and audio systems for persons with hearing loss. Please note that an Accessibility Loan or any other Incentive Loan (Energy Conservation, Asbestos Removal, Lead Paint Control, or New Technology) will not be considered with applications for Facility Purchase, Construction, Renovation, or Manse Loans. Security for Incentive Loans includes a promissory note co-signed by the presbytery, and minutes, certified by the clerk of session, recording session, or congregational action authorizing the borrowing described in the financial plan. For applications or more information regarding Building Accessibility loans or any other building loan from the General Assembly, please contact: Judy Greer, Associate Church Loan Program, Evangelism and Church Development, Presbyterian Church (U.S.A.), 100 Witherspoon St., Rm. 3617, Louisville, KY 40202-1396; phone: (502) 569-5231, fax: 502-569-8323; or Angell Crawford, Senior Administrative Assistant, Church Loan Program; phone: (502) 569-5250.

3. Mary Johnson, *People with Disabilities Explain it All for You: Your Guide to the Public Accommodations Requirements of the Americans with Disabilities Act* (Louisville: Advocado Press, 1992), p. 49.

6. In Service to the Church

1. Rev. Stella Dempski, from comments at a disability consultation with the Commission on Enabling Ministry Services in Louisville in November 1997.

7. A Discussion about Disability

1. From Brett Webb-Mitchell, *Unexpected Guests at God's Banquet* (New York: Crossroad, 1994), pp. 6, 7.

2. Herbert McCabe, *The Teaching of the Catholic Church* (London: Lincoln's Inn Press, Ltd., 1985), p. 42.

Glossary

Board of Pensions—assigned by the General Assembly of the Presbyterian Church (U.S.A.) to oversee the administration of retirement, death, disability, medical, and other benefits for church employees and their families. (www.pcusa.pensions.org)

braille embosser—a special printer that produces braille pages.

curb cut—cuts in sidewalks to allow for wheelchair access to and from the street.

General Assembly—the highest governing body of this church; representative of the unity of the synods, presbyteries, sessions, and congregations of the Presbyterian Church (U.S.A.). (G-13.0101; The Constitution of the Presbyterian Church (U.S.A.), Part II, *Book of Order*, Annotated Edition, 1997–98).

Independent Living Center—a center designed to aid and reinforce independent living among persons with disabilities.

Overture—the means by which a governing body requests some action of change regarding existing church policy by the General Assembly.

paratransit—an alternative means of public transportation for persons with disabilities such as a lift-equipped minivan.

presbytery—a corporate expression of the church consisting of all the churches and ministers of the Word and Sacrament within a certain district. (G-11.0101; The Constitution of the Presbyterian Church (U.S.A.), Part II, *Book of Order*, Annotated Edition, 1997–1998).

synod—the unit of the church's life and mission that consists of not fewer than three presbyteries within a specific geographic region. (G-12.0101; the Constitution of the Presbyterian Church (U.S.A.), Part II, *Book of Order*, Annotated Edition, 1997–1998).

TDD—telecommunication devices for deaf persons.

TTY—teletypewriter.

Appendix 1
The Americans with Disabilities Act
(Pub. L. No. 101-336)*

Title I. Employment

• Employers may not discriminate against an individual with a disability in any aspect of the employment process, including hiring or promotion, if the person is otherwise qualified for the job.

• Before an applicant has been given a job offer, employers may ask about the applicant's ability to perform a job, but may not ask if the applicant has a disability, or subject the applicant to a medical examination or inquiry.

• When asked, employers must provide reasonable accommodation to the known disability of qualified individuals. This includes job restructuring and modification of equipment.

• Employers do not need to provide accommodations that impose an undue hardship on operations. They do, however, need to determine the difficulty or cost of accommodations before attempting to establish an undue hardship defense.

• Employers with fifteen or more employees must comply with Title I requirements.

• A religious organization or entity may give preference in the hiring process to the individuals of a particular religion to perform work connected with the carrying on of its activities.

• Those involved in the religious ministry, such as ministers, priests or rabbis, are not covered by Title I.

Title II: Public Service

Subtitle A: State and Local Governments

• Under the ADA, state and local governments may not discriminate against qualified individuals with disabilities.

• All local jurisdictions (cities, counties, towns,

townships), regardless of size, are required to undertake a self-evaluation and then develop and implement a transition plan.

• All government facilities, services, and communications must be accessible and consistent with the requirements of section 504 of the Rehabilitation Act of 1973, as amended, and with the standards enforced by the Access Board (Architectural and Transportation Barriers Compliance Board).

Subtitle B: Public Transportation

• New public transit buses must be accessible to individuals with disabilities. Transit authorities must provide comparable paratransit or other special transportation services to individuals with disabilities who cannot use fixed route bus service. This service must be provided unless an undue burden would result to the transit authority.

Title III. Public Accommodations

• Title III does not apply to religious organizations or entities controlled by religious organizations, including places of worship.

• Private entities affecting commerce may not discriminate against individuals with disabilities. People with disabilities must be accorded full and equal enjoyment of the goods and services of a place of public accommodation. The categories of public accommodations provided by private entities are as follows:

1. place of lodging (inn, hotel)

2. establishment serving food or drink

3. place of exhibition or entertainment (theater, concert hall)

4. place of public gathering (auditorium, convention center)

5. sales of retail establishment (grocery store, shopping center)

*Key provisions as given in Ginny Thornburgh, *Loving Justice: The ADA and the Religious Community* (Washington, D.C.: National Organization on Disability, 1994), pp. 3–5. Used with permission.

6. service establishment (hospital, gas station, lawyer's office, bank, health care provider, Laundromat)

7. public transportation depots

8. place of public display or collection (library, museum)

9. place of recreation (park, zoo)

10. place of education (nursery, school, college, university)

11. social service center (shelter, food bank)

12. place of exercise or recreation (health spa, golf course, bowling alley)

- It is discriminatory not to allow people with disabilities to have the full and equal enjoyment of any public accommodation.

- Title III of the ADA covers landlords who own and operate places of public accommodation, as well as tenants who lease or sublease the property.

- Eligibility criteria that screen out, or tend to screen out, people with disabilities are prohibited. This includes, for example, requiring the reporting of the existence of a disability on a credit application or requiring a driver's license for identification where a picture identification is all that is necessary.

- Public accommodations are required to make reasonable modifications in policies practices and procedures whenever it is necessary to provide services to a person with a disability, unless the modification would fundamentally alter the nature of the service provided. For example, public accommodations must allow service animals on the premises, even if they prohibit other animals.

- Auxiliary aids and services must be provided to men, women, and children with disabilities, unless an undue burden would result to the public accommodation.

- Physical and communication barriers in existing facilities must be removed, if removal is readily achievable. If not, alternative methods of providing the services must be offered, if they are readily achievable.

- All new construction and alterations of facilities must be accessible.

Title IV: Telecommunications

- Companies offering telephone service to the general public must offer telephone relay services to individuals who use telecommunication devices for the deaf (TDDs) or similar devices.

Title V: Miscellaneous Provisions

- A state is not immune from an action in federal or state court for a violation of the ADA.

- Reasonable attorney's fees, litigation expenses, and costs are recoverable by the prevailing party in an action or administrative proceeding. *Note:* Where applicable, the Civil Rights Act of 1991 provides compensatory and punitive damages and jury trials in ADA proceedings.

- The Access Board has issued the ADA Accessibility Guidelines for Buildings and Facilities, which are available upon request.

- ADA coverage shall extend to the U.S. Senate and House of Representatives.

- For the purposes of the ADA, the term "individual with a disability" does not include an individual who is currently engaging in the illegal use of drugs.

Appendix 2
G.A. Overture 95-46
(*Minutes of the General Assembly, 1995, Part 1, pp. 71, 74, 690-91*)

12.0065

Response: In 1996, the Office of the General Assembly continued to provide braille and large-print versions of the *Book of Order* and *The Book of Confessions*. Computer diskettes were also available for the *Book of Order* and *The Book of Confessions*, as well as the *Annotated Book of Order* and the sexual misconduct paper. No requests were received for material in any other language or alternative format.

12.0066

In 1997, the Office of the General Assembly will work closely with a subcommittee of the Programmatic Resource Coordinating Team to determine the extent of languages and alternative formats already being produced, and those that are still needed by various language communities and Presbyterians with disabilities. The subcommittee works closely with Presbyterians for Disability Concerns to determine methods of alternative modes of communication that will accommodate those with disabilities. Every effort will be made to use the best resources available to the preparation of these materials, and to ensure suitability, insofar as possible, to all Presbyterian persons with disabilities.

12.0067

The 208th General Assembly (1996) made the following comment in reference to this item: "The committee has been reminded of the importance of this referral in the lives of persons with disabilities. We urge that the best available resources be made available to preparation of these materials" (*Minutes*, 1996, Part I, pp. 41–42).

Overture 95–46. On Ministry Tools and Services for Persons with Disabilities—From the Presbytery of Northern New York.

[The Assembly approved Overture 95–46 as amended. See *Minutes*, pp. 71, 74.]

Whereas, God has entered into a covenant with God's people that the eyes of the blind shall be opened, the ears of the deaf unstopped, the lame to walk and the silent to speak and sing (see Matt. 11:4–5); and

Whereas, the Spirit of the living God is given to God's servants for the work of ministry in new and liberating manifestations of life and creation; and

Whereas, the witness in ministry of persons with impairments in vision, hearing, speech and mobility is limited and obstructed by the lack of available tools for ministry and the frustration of limiting ministry by inaccessibility to the means of serving others; and

Whereas, the *Book of Order*, G-4.0403, calls for the Presbyterian Church (U.S.A.) to be as inclusive as possible, especially in reference to people with disabilities; and

Whereas, the 189th General Assembly (1977) of the United Presbyterian Church in the United States of America affirmed in 1977 "that all may enter" into the worship, life, and service of the church in spite of the very disabilities through which Jesus makes the gospel witness (*Minutes*, PC(USA), 1977, Part I, pp. 99–108); and

Whereas, substantial progress has been made in making the *Book of Order* and *The Book of Confessions* available in braille, and their availability serves to underscore the need for a full range of essential ministry resources in alternative media; therefore, be it

Resolved, That the Presbytery of Northern New York Overture the 207th General Assembly (1995) to do the following:

1. Affirm and proclaim the commitment of the Presbyterian Church (U.S.A.) to providing

a. basic tools of ministry in alternative modes of communication to the printed word, for example, braille, tape and computer technology, and signing;

b. accessible meeting places; and

c. translation in the languages of congregations and sister churches with whom we are in mission partnership (where possible).

2. Initiate a study (through a commission appointed at the direction of the General Assembly Council that will include persons who are disabled) to

a. determine the extent and variety of services needed, which shall include an accurate current assessment of the number of persons with disabilities—especially ministers, elders, and church professionals—who require such services in the rendering of their ministries;

b. ascertain sources in society for providing such services as are needed, to explore patterns of present and potential cooperation with secular agencies, and to investigate the costs and means of funding such services;

c. Develop a process for identifying Presbyterian braillists and others who could contribute their skills in technologies of alternative communications and accessibility;

d. report its findings to the 209th General Assembly (1997).

[3. Require that all materials; or a suitable summary thereof—Minutes, resources, curriculum, etc.—produced by the Presbyterian Church (U.S.A.) shall be made available, when requested and in a timely fashion, in one or more of the following alternative formats—large print, audiocassette, braille, or computer disk, with expenditures not to exceed $50,000.

4. Through the General Assembly Council, determine an adequate budget for the above-mentioned commission's work, and seek grants from foundations to help support the work of this commission.]

(Concurrence of Overture 95–46 from the Presbytery of the Western Reserve.)

Appendix 3
Biblical Languages:
Learning Disabilities—Alternative Course of Study

(Policy adopted by the Committee on Preparation for Ministry (CPM), Presbytery of New Brunswick, on May 11, 1998.)

All (educational) requirements of G-14.0310 shall be met except in the following extraordinary circumstances:

G-14.0313a (Extraordinary Circumstances: Educational Requirements)

If the inquirer's or candidate's presbytery judges that there are good and sufficient reasons why certain educational requirements of G-14.0310b(2) b(3) should not be met by an inquirer or candidate, it shall make an exception only by three-fourths vote of the members of presbytery present. A full account of the reasons for such an exception shall be included in the minutes of presbytery and shall be communicated to the presbytery to which the person may be transferred. The successful completion of the course of study specified in such an exception shall fulfill the requirements of G-14.0310b(3).

The *Book of Order* also states: (G-4.0403; Full Participation) "The Presbyterian Church (U.S.A.) shall give full expression to the rich diversity within its membership and shall provide means which will assure a greater inclusiveness leading to wholeness in its emerging life. Persons of all racial ethnic groups, different ages, both sexes, *various disabilities*, . . . shall be guaranteed full participation and access to representation in the decision making of the church."

Our goal and mandate from the CPM was to propose a procedure for reviewing and assessing those inquirers and candidates under our care who have learning disabilities and, when deemed appropriate, outline an alternative course of study for fulfilling the language requirement.

What We Did

• Talked with PC(USA) officials in Louisville: Jerry Houchens, associate, Presbyteries' Cooperative Committees on Examination, Office of the General Assembly; Evelyn Hwang, associate, Resourcing Committees on Preparation for Ministry, National Ministries Division; Patsy Godwin, associate, Theological School Support, Congregational Ministries Division; Dottie Hedgepeth, coordinator, Theological Education.

• Talked with PTS administrators: Kathryn Johnson, director of student relations; Carolyn Nicholson, dean of student affairs; Judy Lang, registrar; James Armstrong, dean of academic affairs.

• Talked with a learning disabilities specialist: Lois Young, executive director of NewGrange School.

• Received materials regarding testing and assessment of persons with disabilities, particularly on dyslexia.

• Researched *Book of Order* requirements, flexibility, and forms of interpretation.

• Read recent articles and legal opinions regarding accommodations for those with learning disabilities in colleges and schools.

• Spoke with administrators and faculty from several area seminaries (Drew University Theological School; Eastern Baptist Theological Seminary (EBTS); New Brunswick Theological Seminary) regarding biblical interpretation and exegesis courses. We also talked with Drew and EBTS officials regarding accommodations in their courses for those with learning disabilities.

• Communicated, as needed, with Committees on Preparation for Ministry (CPM) in other presbyteries.

What We Discovered

There is a wide range of interpretation of the educational requirements from presbytery to presbytery. The denomination does not have specific guidelines or standards in developing an alternative course of study. The decisions reside totally with each presbytery as it assesses each individual. Although PC(USA) officials gave some suggestions, they were very hesitant to give any specific recommendations. It is also important to note that how CPM's interpret the educational requirements of Greek/Hebrew languages and exegesis varies both within the presbyteries and among the Presbyterian and non-Presbyterian seminaries.

We have learned that there is a wide range of differences for those diagnosed with learning disabilities, both in degree and types of dyslexia. Therefore, we are proposing the following assessment procedure.

Assessment

Recommendation for an alternative course of study for Greek or Hebrew (language and exegesis) will be based on existence of an identified, relevant learning disability to be assessed by a special committee as follows:

Assessment Committee

The assessment committee will consist of four members: (1) a person specialized in working with persons having various learning disabilities; (2) a psychologist; (3) a person specialized in teaching biblical language and exegesis; (4) a member of CPM.

If an inquirer or candidate believes himself or herself to have a learning disability that precludes effective study of one or both biblical languages, the inquirer/candidate shall submit, through the CPM chairperson, to the special assessment committee any previous documentation of such disability, and a case history shall be taken in a meeting with the learning disability specialist. The learning disability specialist and the psychologist shall determine together whether any additional testing is required. After any additional testing (if needed), the assessment committee will meet to prepare a recommendation to CPM indicating what level of language work, if any, is realistic to require.

Notes to the above:

- It is likely that in most cases the inquirer/candidate will have adequate previous testing. If not, the cost of testing, and funding, will have to be investigated on a case-by-case basis.

- If the proposal be approved, Lois Young, founder and director of NewGrange School, member and elder of Nassau Church, former member of CPM, has agreed to serve on a volunteer basis as the person specializing in learning disabilities. She is qualified to read reports and do case histories, but not to do any testing.

- If the proposal is approved, Katharine Sakenfeld, CPM member and Princeton Theological Seminary biblical department faculty, minister member of presbytery, has agreed to serve on a volunteer basis as the biblical language specialist.

Recommended Alternative Course of Study

When the above committee recommends that the inquirer/candidate not pursue the usual Greek/Hebrew language requirements, the normal alternative course of study will include the following:

1. A course in exegetical method that does not require the languages. This should normally be B504 Biblical Interpretation at Eastern Baptist Theological Seminary.

> B504 Biblical Interpretation: Through a survey of the history of Biblical interpretation, the principles of biblical hermeneutics will be defined and illustrated. The aim is to assist the student in gaining an appreciation for exegetical method, to develop an awareness of interpretive principles, and to see how these principles and skills may be used in teaching and preaching.

2. A seminary course concentrating on a single Old Testament book, based on English text and concentrating on exegesis, to be chosen in consultation with member #3 of special assessment committee.

3. A seminary course concentrating on a single New Testament book, based on English text and concentrating on exegesis, to be chosen in consultation with member #3 of special assessment committee. . . . The standard ordination examination must be taken, with notification given to the Presbyteries' Cooperative Committee on Examinations for Candidates of the Presbyterian Church (U.S.A.).

Notes to the above:

- None of the three courses can be taken at Princeton Seminary, since Princeton does not offer courses in the categories described.

- If at all possible, decisions concerning course selection should be made on the basis of review of the course syllabus (or a past syllabus that may be slightly modified), rather than on the basis of catalog description alone.

- It will need to be made clear to the inquirer/candidate seeking the exception that any additional costs for tuition at other schools and/or any delays (whether in the ordination process itself or in graduation from seminary because of nontransferable coursework) must be the responsibility of the inquirer/candidate.

- The subcommittee has identified several appropriate courses at the Theological School at Drew University. Courses may also be taken at New Brunswick Theological Seminary, Eastern Baptist Theological Seminary, or another seminary to be agreed upon by CPM on recommendation of person #3 of assessment committee.

Appendix 4
Sample Registration Form
(Designed for the Synod of the Trinity's Annual Retreat for Persons with Disabilities)

Name: _____

Phone: _____

Address: _____

Church: _____

Church phone: _____

Please check all that apply:

☐ $25 Registration fee **or** ☐ $75 Total fee enclosed. (Please make check payable to Synod of the Trinity)

☐ Event scholarship help needed. Amount requested: _____

☐ I will arrive by private car.

☐ I will need to be picked up at the ☐ bus station; ☐ train station.

☐ Please send information about other transportation.[*]

My needs include the following:

☐ Wheelchair accessible room.

☐ Help with bathing.

☐ Help with meals.

☐ Help with dressing.

☐ Diet restrictions: _____

☐ Other: _____

☐ I am blind; ☐ have a dog; and ☐ need materials in braille.

☐ I am hearing impaired, and ☐ need an interpreter.

☐ I have difficulty walking distances.

☐ I have difficulty climbing steps.

☐ Yes ☐ No   I have attended the Retreat before.

☐ Yes ☐ No   I need a caregiver.

☐ I will bring my own caregiver. (*Note:* Caregivers are asked to complete a Registration Form for themselves and contribute the total fee.)

In order for us to serve you better, is there anything else we need to know about you?

[*]This would include paratransit or other accessible transportation needs.

About the Commission Members and Staff

Ann Madsen Dailey, M.A. C.C.C.Spl, is a speech/language pathologist who has worked with clients limited in communication skills. The clients range in age from preschool children to veterans receiving treatment in VA hospitals. The areas of treatment included children with delay or disorders in language processing, particularly in the auditory modality; hearing impaired; adults who suffered strokes; and speech development delay. She is an elder in the Presbyterian Church in Sudbury, Massachusetts, and actively serving on committees in the Presbytery of Boston.

Sharon Kutz-Mellem is the former managing editor of the critically acclaimed disability publication *The Disability Rag*. She has more than twenty years' experience in the area of disability, ranging from caregiver and advocate to family member and person with a disability. She has served as a leadership team member and co-moderator of Presbyterians for Disabilities Concerns and is the editor of their newsletter. She was a member of the Disability Advisory Panel of the Louisville Presbytery and is a member of Crescent Hill Presbyterian Church in Louisville, Kentucky.

Sue Sterling Montgomery was ordained to the ministry in the PC(USA) in 1997. She has served as a pastor of smaller membership churches in Indiana, Illinois, and Pennsylvania. In 1983, Sue began an additional ministry as chaplain at Polk Center, a residential training facility for persons with mental retardation. Sue is active in advocacy ministries locally, and nationally on the Advocacy Committee for Women's Concerns of the General Assembly. She is married to the Rev. Jay E. Montgomery and the mother of a son, Joel, age twelve.

Darlene Paul currently is a sign language interpreter at the University of Nebraska and Lincoln Heritage Presbyterian Church in Lincoln, Nebraska. She has been a teacher and active in the field for more than twenty years. She is a member of the National Registry of Interpreters for the Deaf and holds the highest rating possible in the state of Nebraska.

William J. Richard Jr., Presbyterian minister retired, was born blind from congenital glaucoma. Educated in schools for the blind (K–6), public school (7–12), Harvard College, and Union Theological Seminary, New York, Bill has served the church as pastor of three small congregations, as campus minister for twenty-four years, and has been active contributor to presbytery, synod, and GA committees. He was commissioner to several synods and two general assemblies. He has been a member of Presbyterians for Disability Concerns/Leadership Team, PHEWA, and most recently the Commission on Enabling Ministry Services. His ministry style is partnership. He is fluent in braille and has worked with three Seeing Eye guide dogs for more than thirty years. Bill and his wife Anne Marie (Rie) live in Addison, Vermont.

Diane Wheeler, commission chairperson, is an elder, member, and clerk of session for Western Presbyterian Church, Palmyra, New York; member of General Assembly Council (class 1999), Presbyterian Church (U.S.A.); graduate New York State University, Albany, New York; Library of Congress–certified braille transcriber; volunteer Meals on Wheels, United Way of Wayne County; Palmyra Library Board president.

Gladys Williams, Ph.D., is a retired college teacher of English and American literature. She has served the church as elder and chair of stewardship and evangelism committees and as a member of finance, outreach, and preparation for ministry. She was director of the Black Education Resource Development Project, an ecumenically supported church school curriculum in the early 1980s, and was a trustee of the Presbyterian Foundation from 1990 to 1996 and a member of the executive committee of the Foundation in 1995–1996. Gladys is married to Russell Spry Williams, now an honorably retired minister of the Word and Sacrament. They are the parents of two adult children. Their daughter, Anne, is hearing impaired.

Annie Wu King was born in China, where she contracted polio before she was one year old. After graduating from the University of Pennsylvania in Oriental Studies, she taught for more than ten years at a Christian university in Java, returning to complete a master's degree in social work at the University of Louisville. She has worked at an independent living center for persons with disabilities, with responsibilities in accessible housing and counseling, and as a licensed clinical social worker; she also works in private practice as a therapist. Currently, she is a member of the staff of Women's Ministries, National Ministries Division of the Presbyterian Church (U.S.A.), in Louisville, Kentucky. Annie is a member of Crescent Hill Presbyterian Church.

Agnes Young, LICSW, elder at Hartford Street Presbyterian Church in Malick, Massachusetts, is currently the chair for the Committee on Representation, Presbytery of Boston, and is also a member of the leadership team of Presbyterians for Disabilities Concerns (PHEWA). Prior to retirement, Agnes was employed as an administrator at the Massachusetts Department of Transition Services, with the responsibility for the implementation of the Federal Rehabilitation Act of 1973, sections 503 and 504, and ADA. This responsibility included serving as the hearing officer and rendering decisions resulting from complaints filed by disabled employees and for clients receiving services from Human Services providers.

About the Photographers

Nancy Anne Dawe is a widely published writer and photojournalist who lives on Seabrook Island, South Carolina. Her photography appears in books, magazines, newspapers, calendars, various business publications and brochures, and on posters and greeting cards. She is author and photographer of *I Lift My Eyes to the Hills: Stories of Faith and Joy from Appalachia* (Minneapolis: Augsburg Fortress, 1992).

Lydia Gans retired from her first career as a mathematics professor and turned to photojournalism. Her publications include *To Live with Grace and Dignity* (Horsham, PA: LRP Publications, 1994) and *Sisters, Brothers, and Disability: A Family Album* (Minneapolis: Fairview Press, 1997). She is now working on a new book and freelancing for various newspapers and magazines.